the FARMER'S CODE

Mike C. Young

THE
FARMER'S
CODE

HOW *Legacies* ARE BUILT

Forbes | Books

Published by Forbes Books, Charleston, South Carolina.
An imprint of Advantage Media Group.

Forbes Books is a registered trademark, and the Forbes Books colophon is a trademark of Forbes Media, LLC.

Printed in the United States of America.

10 9 8 7 6 5 4 3 2 1

ISBN: 978-1-64225-663-5 (Hardcover)
ISBN: 978-1-64225-662-8 (eBook)

Library of Congress Control Number: 2023911055

Cover design by Matthew Morse.
Layout design by Matthew Morse.

This custom publication is intended to provide accurate information and the opinions of the author in regard to the subject matter covered. It is sold with the understanding that the publisher, Forbes Books, is not engaged in rendering legal, financial, or professional services of any kind. If legal advice or other expert assistance is required, the reader is advised to seek the services of a competent professional.

Since 1917, Forbes has remained steadfast in its mission to serve as the defining voice of entrepreneurial capitalism. Forbes Books, launched in 2016 through a partnership with Advantage Media, furthers that aim by helping business and thought leaders bring their stories, passion, and knowledge to the forefront in custom books. Opinions expressed by Forbes Books authors are their own. To be considered for publication, please visit **books.Forbes.com**.

This book is dedicated to an angel, a matriarch, a friend, and a teacher. She goes by many names, including Mom, Gunk, Grandma, and GG. This book wouldn't have ever been conceived without her love and leadership to our family.

This book is dedicated to my grandmother, Vivian Verda Wegis. She turned one hundred in November of 2022 and was a big inspiration in the writing of this book.

LEGACY IS NOT LEAVING SOMETHING FOR PEOPLE.
IT'S LEAVING SOMETHING IN PEOPLE.

Peter Strople

contents

part one

KNOWING YOUR IDENTITY (ME)

part two
ESTABLISH LOVING RELATIONSHIPS (US)

part three
IMPACT THE WORLD (THEM NOW)

part four
LIVING YOUR LEGACY (THEM TO COME)

acknowledgments

Writing a book is hard. Yet it is also one of the most rewarding things I've ever done. I have loved the process. This book would not be possible without the family that I was lucky enough to be born into. These are the people I work with, live with, and play with. They are the people who ground me and build me up at the same time. Each person brings something special and unique to this family. Just as every puzzle piece is unique in a puzzle, our family is the same. And without each one of them, we wouldn't be whole.

It starts with my grandmother, Vivian, the matriarch and the one who really instilled the values in each one of us of what it means to live and leave a legacy. She and my grandfather were the second generation of our family tree: G2. Then there is G3: my mom and dad—Patti and Richard—and uncle and aunt—Rick and Mary. This is the crew that made G4 (my generation) live as siblings and not cousins. They are the group who taught us "work hard and play hard, together" is how life was meant to be lived.

Then there is my generation, my brothers and sister and of course their spouses: Jeff and Melissa, Greg and Gina, and Joe and Jane.

These are my partners for life. I can't think of a better crew to continue to live the "work hard and play hard, together" motto with.

Then, of course, there is G5: the next generation. I wrote this book for them. This is a group of first and second cousins that love each other the same way I love my cousins—as siblings. Emma, Halle, Jacob, Aiden, Sydney, Reagan, Kate, Antone, and Bennett, we can't wait to see how you flourish and how you pass this legacy to G6.

And, of course, my line of the family tree wouldn't be possible without the love of my life, my rock, and my biggest cheerleader— my wife, Jennifer. Thank you for supporting me through this whole process. I never could have done this without your love, support, and critical eye.

Beyond my family there is a huge support team that is always there for me and always encouraging me when I do stuff way out of the ordinary and way out of most people's comfort zone. I've got a small group of close friends that have been listening to me grumble about this book for a few years now. They are my personal board of directors, my confidants, my YPO buddies, and some of my closest friends. I couldn't imagine walking this earth without them. Thank you to my S|K 8 brothers: Antonio, Daren, Jeff A., Jeff M., Jim, Ray, and Mike.

The challenge and the spark of an idea for this book came from a group that I belong to named Alder (alder.co). It is a group of community leaders who are committed to living a legacy that makes the country freer and better for future generations. Thank you to Michael and Maria for your encouragement and nudge to take an idea and share it with the world.

Many of the ideas in this book came from many hours and lessons learned in two organizations: the California Ag Leadership Foundation and Discovery Church Bakersfield. I am very grateful to have had the opportunity to be a fellow in Ag Leadership. Class thirty-five is, by far, the best and brightest class to go through the program. I am eternally grateful for the founders, Dean Brown and J. G. Boswell, for having the foresight to found, seed, and watch flourish the best leadership development program in the world—a program that is fifty-two years old as of this publishing and growing.

Pastor Jason Hanash of Discovery Church Bakersfield is, in my mind, one of the foremost leadership development coaches I know, along with being a heart-led, grace-filled, fiery man of God. He can easily break down complex leadership topics and teach the masses through the lens of the Bible on how to institute them into our own lives. I am grateful that God lit the path for me to cross paths with Pastor Jason. Much of what he has taught me has landed in this book.

Last, this book would not be possible without my editors and publisher. If you are the type of person who writes and has more red squiggles under their words than most on a sheet, you can imagine the frustration of this crew. Thank you for making this book readable! Most importantly I want to thank Jim House and Heidi Scott. They have become like family to me, and their partnership with me and willingness to challenge me through this process are what made this book possible. I am eternally grateful for the two of you.

about the author

MIKE C. YOUNG is an author/writer, husband, father, and leader of the fourth-generation family office Wegis & Young, which is rooted in agriculture and real estate. Grounded in integrity, he works with three generations of shareholders instilling principles of love, respect, and honest business practices leading to profitable futures. His mission is to lead with integrity, challenge with purpose, and cultivate compassion and faith while making a meaningful difference in the lives of others that will create a better world for generations to come.

Mike's success comes from his deep set of values and his insatiable appetite to learn. He has many leadership roles within his industry and community. He is an accredited iEQ9 Enneagram practitioner, which he uses as a tool in mentoring and coaching emerging leaders so that he can help empower them to leave a legacy.

Mike lives in Bakersfield, California, with his wife, Jennifer. Together they have three adult children.

Learn more about Mike at mikecyoung.com.

introduction

I am the kind of person who always has a "thing." My family teases me about it all the time. Whether I'm training for an endurance event or researching new trends in agriculture and business, I am not the kind of person who sits still.

So it was easy to forgive my family as they rolled their eyes a little bit when I shared my plan to write a book. "Why on earth would you want to write about us?" my mother asked. "We're just a regular family. Nobody wants to read anything about us."

While I completely agree with her that we are, indeed, a regular family with regular lives full of regular problems, collectively we are more. We don't always appreciate what we have, because we don't know any different. There is something unique and, in many ways, remarkable about our family. And this is why I wanted to write a book.

For one thing we have kept our family business going for four generations, going on five. And not just staying afloat, but rather growing and thriving. We have weathered storms (literally and meta-phorically) that have crippled many businesses in our industry. We have grown from a single owner/operator—my great-grandfather—to a multimillion-dollar company with a diversified asset base. We have proven that our business model can withstand the kind of strain that is routinely taking down many other family businesses.

On top of all of this, we have woven into the fabric of our business a focus on charity, love, grace, and acceptance that has become synonymous in our community with our family names, Wegis and Young. What has been built by my family is something we are proud to pass down to the next generation, "G5," as we affectionately call our kids. And people ask me all the time, "How did you do it?"

My purpose in writing this book is to show how you, too, can build a legacy that will positively impact the world.

As the title suggests, our family business is rooted in the agricultural industry. We started out as farmers, and the lessons we learned from working the land have been crucial to the legacy we have built. I decided to take a more critical look at those lessons and the influence they had. Rather than writing a dull, philosophical book that would likely gather dust rather than readers, I decided to use the farmer's code as a metaphor for aspects of building a legacy. This metaphor could have taken on encyclopedic proportions if I went too far, so I have only used this metaphor as a guide for the discussion. This book is intended to inspire thought, imagination, and goals.

SUCCESS LEAVES CLUES.

Success leaves clues. My task was to find those clues, follow them, and explore what they meant in terms of a legacy. As I did so, I realized that a legacy is a sustained commitment to an idea. To something that is not in your face every single day. It is knowing that your commitment to the future goes way beyond you.

One theme that you'll see in these pages is that my life centers on Christ. Because of this you will see themes of Christianity throughout the book. This is intentional, as I could not write an authentic book without including this huge piece of my identity. I have also included themes from other faith systems and religions. My hope is that my readers will approach this with an open mind and an open heart and that their own, individual spiritual nature is uplifted because of what is included.

Living and leaving a legacy requires making the right choices, things that don't require talent. You can choose to smile, choose to show up early, choose to work harder, choose to be loyal, choose to be faithful, choose to be dedicated, choose to persevere, choose to have tenacity. These choices will take you much farther in life than talent ever will, and they will leave an impression on generations to come because you have set a standard for living.

Don't think it's easy. There is always conflict—especially within families. It is part of human nature, and experts say it's impossible to completely remove it from any family business. That's because family conflict can stem from childhood resentment or anger from which adults have sometimes never fully healed. If left unaddressed, those sources of conflict exert tremendous forces of separation on the family and pull it apart. It keeps family members from giving each other the benefit of the doubt or from being able to express love and care and concern for one another—the secret to a lasting legacy.

Ultimately, a legacy isn't a thing you leave behind; it's how you shape the future of others. My own grandfather and grandmother raised their family and nurtured them as much as they nurtured their legacy, but they didn't even know it. They weren't perfect, by any means, but they loved and adored their grandkids, and I believe that was the key that unlocked the amazing legacy they built.

This book is divided into four sections: Me, Us, Them Now, and Them to Come. It is important that we become healthy and fully functional before we can influence anyone else to do the same, so I begin by exploring ways you, personally, can do your part to be the best *you* possible.

With that covered, I then introduce the idea of "Us," meaning your inner circle of people closest to you. For me this includes my wife and children, my siblings and their families, my parents, aunts and uncle, grandparents, and a small circle of friends. These are the people closest to me and the people I have the most access to in terms of influence and being influenced. You might include very close friends or "adopted" family members in your own inner circle.

The next level is our wider local circle, which I call "Them Now." These are the people you work with, associate with, enjoy socially, even if only occasionally. It also includes people you haven't ever met but live tangential to such as colleagues in your industry, community members in your hometown, social media connections, etc. This is your expanded world and one that you have the ability to affect in a positive (or negative) way.

Finally, I cover the group I call "Them to Come." As you have probably guessed, this is where the legacy comes in. These are the people you will never know but that stand to gain the very most from your actions today. The outer ripple in the pond is always the biggest, which leads us to consider how our tiny actions can have an effect on people we can't see. This is the group I am most excited about and the whole reason I wrote this book.

I love to read. You will find many of my favorite authors and favorite books quoted in this book. Many books I go back to again and again to relearn and stay sharp on their concepts. And with that I encourage you to mark up this book, dog-ear the pages, highlight words and sentences, and scribble notes in the margin. And by all means share what you learn! Most importantly learn The Code and develop your own code to live a legacy that will last well beyond you.

WEGIS - ETCHEVERRY - YOUNG

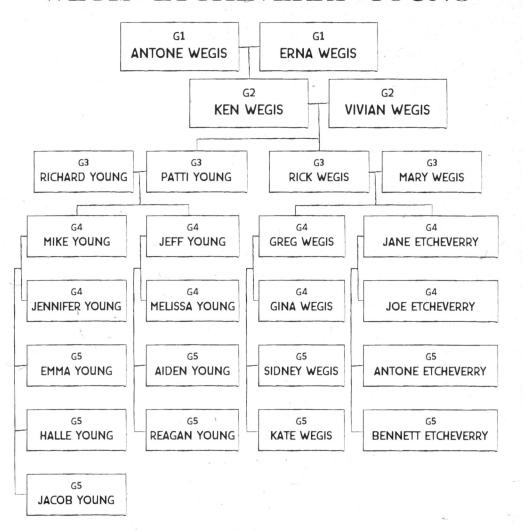

LD A POSITIVE, PERMANENT *legacy*

OUGH DELIBERATE, *daily choices.*

PART 1

Knowing Your Identity (Me)

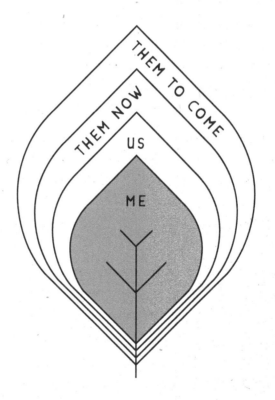

IF YOU WANT TO CHANGE THE WORLD,
START WITH YOURSELF.

Mahatma Gandhi

one

Planting

The Farmer's Code

As farmers, our family depends on the land, just as we have for over four generations. Every season we plant a new crop. For four generations we have grown products like rice, sugar beets, alfalfa, wheat, cotton, garlic, carrots, broccoli, tomatoes, cucumbers, grapes, cherries, citrus, almonds, and pistachios. While the crops we grow have changed over the generations, one thing never has—our dedication and commitment to hard work, to our employees, to our community, and most importantly to our family.

Planting a new crop is like adopting a growth mindset. We plant a seed and nurture it with care and concern over its vitality. Similarly, we plant and nurture seeds of improvement in ourselves as we walk the path of personal growth and development. We accept and learn about new ideas and concepts that we believe will bear fruit one day. These are the "seeds" we plant in ourselves. We care for them with continued study and practice, finding better ways to help them grow through time. As we do this, we develop a "code" for ourselves of best practices that we live by and that we can pass on to the future generations as our legacy to them.

Developing that legacy takes time, preparation, and tools. It is work that begins now, not later in life. A legacy is meant to be lived.

How It All Began

Luck is where time and opportunity meet.

For me that happened on a dusty playground in rural Kern County, California, circa 1932. My grandmother Vivian, whom we all now call GG, was ten years old and in fourth grade. She was standing her ground on a swing set while a bully named Billy was trying to knock her off it. Along came a boy with a big head and big ears who knocked Billy to the ground and told him to stop picking on girls. From that day on, a friendship was born.

The boy was my grandfather Ken Wegis. My grandmother, who is one hundred now, still says to this day that the reason she married Ken was because he stood up to the "bully named Billy."

GG didn't have an easy life growing up. There wasn't much love in her house. Her father was an alcoholic, and there were times when she would move schools five times in one year because her father was floating from one job loss to the next. Despite that instability, she had a spirit of perseverance.

She persevered when her father told her she couldn't go to college because girls "can't do that." She persevered when her father wouldn't support her marriage to my grandfather, not even going to her wedding because he was too busy chasing his next wild dream. She persevered when their first home as a married couple was a trailer with cardboard walls and no plumbing. She persevered when my grandfather passed away at the young age of seventy-two.

Life was never easy for my grandmother growing up, and yet I never knew any of this until I started to write this book. She always chose to focus on the positive things in her past and not the negative.

Honestly, she was basically given a garbage bag at the beginning of her life. But she didn't pass the garbage bag along to the next generation. She passed along a code to the next generation, and with that code our legacy began. She passed to us love, acceptance, positivity, and strength.

Knowing Your Identity

The notion of self-awareness is crucial before one can even begin to think about leaving a legacy. Self-awareness seems like a bit of an esoteric concept, but basically all I mean is that you have enough presence of mind and insight to know your strengths, limitations, talents, weaknesses, and essential personality traits. It also includes knowing how other people see you. Once you figure out who you are, it will dictate where you will go in life and what you want to do at your core. As Dr. Daniel Goleman, who authored one of the first books on emotional intelligence, said, "The more socially intelligent you are, the happier and more robust and more enjoyable your relationships will be."[1]

---

1   Daniel Goleman, BrainyQuote, accessed June 6, 2023, https://www.brainyquote.com/quotes/daniel_goleman_585898.

When we develop greater self-awareness, it is easy to understand who we are and what is important to us. We can step outside of ourselves; we begin to see how to live our best lives and more effectively serve those around us. Self-aware people can forge stronger, more authentic relationships with others, while those who lack this skill tend to alienate and even offend those around them.

IF YOU LACK SELF—KNOWLEDGE AND SELF—AWARENESS, YOU WILL GREATLY HANDICAP YOUR ADVANTAGE IN THE WORKPLACE, THE LOVE SPACE, THE FRIEND SPACE, AND THE FAMILY SPACE.

Cornell University did a business school study[2] on the key predictors in business success, and self-awareness was at the top of the list. I believe this is true in any relationship. If you lack self-knowledge and self-awareness, you will greatly handicap your advantage in the workplace, the love space, the friend space, and the family space. As psychologist Abby Medcalf stated, "What self-awareness does is allow you to see your natural [shortcomings] and how those most impact others around you."[3]

The more you know yourself, the more you understand your blind spots and the more you understand your gifts. You can monitor

---

2   Victor Lipman, "All Successful Leaders Need This Quality: Self-Awareness," November 18, 2013, https://www.forbes.com/sites/victorlipman/2013/11/18/all-successful-leaders-need-this-quality-self-awareness/?sh=3a50f9ac1f06.

3   Abby Medcalf, quoted in "4 Surefire Signs That a Person Lacks Self-Aware-ness—And Why That's a Big Issue in Relationships," Well + Good, February 2022, accessed June 6, 2023, https://www.wellandgood.com/signs-low-self-awareness/#:~:text=realize%20is%20broken.-,%E2%80%9CWhat%20self%2Dawareness%20does%20is%20allow%20you%20to%20see%20your,their%20way%2C%E2%80%9D%20she%20adds.

the way you act, think, and feel rather than running on autopilot. Without any sense of self-awareness, you tend to bang guardrail to guardrail through life.

Lack of self-awareness is self-deception, and signs of self-deception can include defensiveness, microfocus on the short term, mistrust of others, compulsive need to control, lack of empathy or sympathy, drama seeking, taking more credit than deserved, arrogance, playing victim, inability to admit wrongs, inflexibility, talking incessantly, gossip, negativity, and pride.

There is so much hope if you just realize you have any of these behaviors. I've known people who would walk into a crowded room and within minutes had unconsciously offended everyone there. That takes almost Herculean effort, and yet they haven't the slightest idea! (By the way, the fact that you're reading this book is a pretty good sign you are not one of these people.)

I believe that even the most self-absorbed narcissists can change. So can the most defeated, lemon-sucking pessimists. If you see yourself as a person who is stupid or as someone who doesn't have talent, then that's who you become. It doesn't matter if you read the right books, listen to the right podcasts, or watch the right speakers. If negativity is a part of your identity, that's who you will portray in the world.

To me emotional immaturity is directly connected to a brokenness of the soul or a deceitful heart. We aren't born that way, but it is developed over time through our upbringing, our circumstances, and our own individual traumas. And we all have trauma—some of us have little "t" trauma and some of us big "T" Trauma.

The biggest difference between emotionally mature people and emotionally immature people is self-awareness. Self-awareness leads to emotional maturity.

The first step is to acknowledge that you must improve your self-awareness if you are going to grow. Then the second step is to understand that belief will raise you. Your fears must submit to your beliefs. Changing yourself means not letting the world change you or dictate who you are. You know the old saying, I'm sure: feed your dreams and starve your doubts. Your beliefs will lift you—not an arrogant belief, but a confident belief.

When you believe that "more" is possible for your life, "more" comes into your life.

I was recently at Target, and the guy in line behind me had a T-shirt on that said, "Future Billionaire."

I asked him, "Are you there yet?"

He said (with a huge smile on his face), "Nope, but I'm trying!"

He made the choice to live his day with a growth mindset, one that will get him to his dreams. And after that brief interaction, I believe he will get there too.

Principles of a Growth Mindset

One of my favorite authors is John C. Maxwell. He is an expert in leadership and self-development. His book *The 15 Invaluable Laws of Growth* is one of my all-time most gifted books and one that I refer to often.

In it he teaches that there are fifteen principles that are certain to help a person grow. Awareness is number two, just behind Intentionality. I first picked this book up when I was early in my leadership journey. We had one small child, and I was just beginning to step into leadership roles within our business and the agricultural industry. I tried to apply a new law from this book each week into my life. I have learned that, while I can never do all fifteen laws well, knowing them and understanding them has made me more self-aware of who I am and what my capabilities are.

These laws remain true, whether you practice them or not. Much like the law of gravitation, if you don't act on it, it is still true. So for me, applying these truths to my life has made me better understand myself, which includes my strengths and weaknesses.

By now I'd be willing to bet that most people have come across the term "growth mindset." This refers to the belief that you can always do more with what you have right now. This is directly opposite a "fixed mentality," or the belief that if you are not good at something now, you will never be good at it. The classic, glass-half-empty-versus-half-full metaphor.

If you like, think of life as a series of doors. When one closes another always opens. If you have your mind set on a specific outcome, you might miss the incredible opportunities that lie behind the doors you are not opening because you are afraid to try. When you push yourself to try new things and learn more, you will very likely find something even more amazing that takes you somewhere you never imagined. Your mindset determines what happens next.

When I First Developed a Growth Mindset

My grandfather, Ken Wegis, was a captain of the agriculture industry in the state of California. He influenced me in more ways than I can explain, with the most crucial lessons having to do with my own sense of self-worth and confidence. Grandpa was always in the forefront of his field and looked ten to fifteen years ahead. He sat on many boards, read all that he could about his industry, and kept close tabs on the influences that would make his business successful or take it down. This foresight saved his company time and time again from ruin.

He was not attached to tradition, as so many farmers are. Rather, he sought out the latest and newest information, accepting that change was critical to survival.

Watching him was key to my personal development. Seeing my uncle and my dad have the same growth mindset inspired me. When the torch was passed, I knew I needed the same self-development work to stay ahead of what was coming next.

Sometimes, having a growth mindset means doing things that are out of your comfort zone. Growing up on a farm like I did was wonderful in so many ways, but I was the kid who hated getting dirty. I never particularly liked working on the ranch, but it's what our family did. So I did too.

But when I was in college, I really fell in love with politics. Because this is where I learned that politics plays a crucial role in shaping the direction of society, as it determines the allocation of resources, distribution of power and implementation of policies that directly impact the lives of individuals, making it indispensable in achieving social progress and insuring a just and equitable future.

I came home to work on the farm for a summer after I graduated while I tried to figure out what I wanted to do with the rest of my life. I figured I would go to Washington, DC, and maybe work on the Hill. I had also been dating this amazing girl but was pretty sure she didn't want to follow me back East and leave her family all behind in California. Honestly, I was floundering with making any clear decisions about my life.

Grandpa had just been diagnosed with pancreatic cancer, but he was still going to work every day. One day we were driving his old Ford station wagon back home on Seventh Standard Road from a trip to Bakersfield, which is about a half an hour away from the farm. I don't remember why we had gone to town, but I remember this conversation like it was yesterday.

Just as we passed a grove of almond trees, he turned to me and said, "You know what? You need to marry that girl. I know you don't like getting dirty, but you need to come back home for good and work with your dad and uncle."

This really got my attention, because he didn't make a habit of giving advice like that, and it changed the course of the rest of my whole life. For me the very idea of making a career as a farmer was out of my comfort zone. But Grandpa was my hero, and when your hero says something, you just do it. I decided right then that I would get married, join the family business, and make a life there.

He lived less than six months after that before he died. He was not at our wedding, but his influence has continued with me and my family to this day.

The farmer's code is something that takes time and preparation. It doesn't matter what stage of life we are in, we can all begin to live and leave a legacy. Start figuring out your code now!

Pruning

TRUTH AND COURAGE AREN'T ALWAYS COMFORTABLE,
BUT THEY ARE NEVER A WEAKNESS.

Brené Brown

The Farmer's Code

Our family has grown almonds for generations. At the end of each harvest, we have to go in and prune the almond trees to create space for light to shine. As we do this, we also remove dead and diseased branches so that the following years' crops will have a better chance to grow. This is a difficult process that sometimes involves making painful decisions to keep the tree healthy. It very often isn't easy to cut away parts of the tree, knowing in the short term we won't have a great crop, but it will be better for the trees' production in the long term.

Likewise, when traveling down the road of self-development and legacy building, we have to prepare ourselves for growth by removing the impurities and obstacles that stand in the way. Legacies are built when we persistently address our own flaws in hopes of positive development. It can be a slow and painstaking process, but it is so critical. With every flaw that is removed, we are guaranteed a direct impact on the outcome. For almonds the yields are healthier and higher. For people they are deeper and longer lasting.

It's All in the Mind

Self-pruning is one of the hardest things we must do when we begin to build a path of self-development. We all have flaws, inside and out. As you might imagine, there is a spectrum of severity as to where our personality flaws fall, and they might fluctuate depending on the context of every situation. Trivial personality flaws might include a tendency to show up late or talk too loudly in social settings. Significant concerns include traits like being selfish, neglectful, or even abusive. Our attitude around those flaws is what determines the type of legacy we leave, because embracing the flaws doesn't allow the more authentic version of us to grow.

> *A story that has been told for many years tells of a young couple moving into a new neighborhood. The young wife sits with her husband over breakfast that first day in their new home and sees her neighbor hanging laundry on the line next door. She comments to her husband that the neighbor doesn't know how to wash her clothes very well, because they are still dirty. Her husband looks out the window, shrugs, and goes back to eating.*
>
> *After that, every time the neighbor hangs her laundry, the young wife watches in disgust, commenting to her husband about what the state of affairs must be like in that home if this is the woman's*

level of cleanliness. This goes on until one morning the woman looks out the window and gasps. "Look!" she calls to her husband. "The neighbor finally figured out how to wash her clothes correctly. Everything is clean!"

Her husband chuckles and says, "Well actually, there was never a problem with our neighbor. I just cleaned our windows yesterday."

How easy is it to pass judgment on others when we, ourselves are imperfect. As the Savior said, "And why do you look at the speck in your brother's eye, but do not consider the plank in your own eye?" (Matthew 7:3 NKJV).

When I think of self-pruning and personality traits, I envision doing work on myself and cultivating a sense of self-awareness. It's about understanding your own strengths and weaknesses and allowing this work to influence how you might treat others, either as a manager or a team member.

EQ

The term emotional intelligence, or EQ, has been around since it was coined by researchers Peter Salovey and John D. Mayer in 1990. They defined it in the *Imagination, Cognition and Personality Journal* (yes, there is such a thing) as "a form of social intelligence that involves the ability to monitor one's own and others' feelings and emotions, to discriminate among them, and to use this information to guide one's thinking and action."[4]

---

4   Peter Salovey and John D. Mayer, "Emotional Intelligence," *Imagination, Cognition and Personality* 9, no. 3: 185–211, https://doi.org/10.2190/DUGG-P24E-52WK-6CDG.

Since then the science and study of emotional intelligence has become ubiquitous in the world of self-improvement, counseling, and leadership. A key predictor of success in life is self-awareness, without question. If you are armed with that, you will not bang guardrail to guardrail through relationships, work, and everything else in your life.

I think one of the biggest mistakes you can make in life is to presume you actually know all there is to know about yourself. Using assessment tools will help with self-awareness, which is a key predictor in the success of leaving a lasting legacy. There are countless assessments available. Personally, I like the Enneagram. I find it to be an uncannily accurate personality typing system that centers on nine basic personality types. One of these types is what we gravitate toward and adopt in childhood, just as a way to feel safe. It is our go-to to protect ourselves and to navigate the new world of relationships. But we all have elements of every one of the nine types, each with an unconscious motivation.

I like the Enneagram because, unlike many other personality assessments, it is actionable, accessible, and quick to understand at a basic level. It doesn't just tell you what you do, but instead why you do it. It reveals motivations, both conscious and unconscious, and because of that, you can see what's going on below the waterline that drives the way you act, think, and feel above the waterline. The Enneagram also tells you what you are like when you are under stress. This gets to the heart of better understanding ourselves, our story, so that we can be our truest, most authentic self.

With that being said, I like anything that helps people develop self-knowledge. The important thing is finding a way to learn about yourself on a deeper level.

The better you are at who you are, the better you'll do at what you do. So unpack who you are.

Character Sustains You

Self-awareness is central to developing a solid character. Your character sustains you. If we look at biblical examples, Noah did what was right, even if he was alone. Joseph endured despite the circumstances in Egypt. Moses was brave and stood by his people.

Your character will keep you grounded. While charisma will get you in the door, character is what will keep you there. You must have ethics in business and life. In our family company, we treat everyone like they are family. I know a lot of companies say this. After all, it's easy for management to believe things about their company, but unless those philosophies trickle down to every single employee, they are simply ideas and not reality. I wanted to find out if the employees in our company actually felt like they were family, so I had a chat with one of our longest-term staff members, Rhonda. She has been our company controller for more than a decade and shared her very personal experience with this concept.

> THE BETTER YOU ARE AT WHO YOU ARE, THE BETTER YOU'LL DO AT WHAT YOU DO. SO UNPACK WHO YOU ARE.

Thirteen years ago, I lost my job as an accountant in the oil industry, so I put my resume out online. By the grace of God, I found out that Wegis & Young was hiring. I drove out to Button-willow—an hour drive, thinking the whole time, "I don't want to work all the way out here, but I need a job."

I walked in for the interview, and all the guys were sitting around this table with their dogs all around, and dog hair was every-

where. I thought, "OK, this is different. But heck, accounting is accounting, no matter where you're at."

They hired me on the spot, and I started the next day and learned immediately how generous and wonderful these people were. Richard Young said, "OK, tomorrow you can be a little bit late, because I want you to go pick out a company car. And feel free to replace everything in this office. If you need a computer, printer, whatever, just get it."

I'm thinking, "Is this real?" But I felt welcome from the moment I started. I was like family.

We went from just two managed accounts to thirty-four. I have seen that legacy of generosity trickle down five generations now. They're very compassionate, and they genuinely believe in the value of everyone being a family member. And if you're a family member, they love you, unconditionally.

Just a few weeks later, my husband left me out of the blue after thirty-five years. I don't want to make this personal, but he basically walked out the door to go to work and never came back. If that had happened in my prior job, I would have been completely alone. I was working in a snake pit of an office environment. I would've had to go through that whole big mess without any support. But here, they were a huge support from the moment it happened. That's the type of people they are. They wrapped me in their arms and made sure I was OK. I have been working for fifty years and have never seen anything like it. But more importantly it made me want to live and be the example they had been for me to those I love and those around me.

Growth Comes Out of Failures

Albert Einstein said, "You cannot solve a problem with the same thinking that created the problem."

It takes courage and faith to grow. I love adventure, and all the great explorers took on huge challenges, not knowing what would happen. Sir Edmund Hillary, Marco Polo, Amelia Earhart. The list goes on. Their vision for what could happen and what they could become was more important than any random worry about what could go wrong, and this is part of why they became legends.

God can help you grow in your character. Once we are no longer chained to our need for control and safety, He can heal with His bravery, His love, His guidance, and His protection. What we once thought would bring us destruction He uses to build a foundation.

The movie *The Pursuit of Happyness* reminds us that it's not just one mistake that determines our future. In most cases it is rather a series of continual choices made over time that molds and makes the person. It raises questions about ethics, morality, and right and wrong. In the movie Will Smith gives an excellent performance as Chris Gardner, and the story is truly inspiring. We follow Chris and his young son as they hit rock bottom, experiencing divorce to home-lessness and unemployment. I like this movie because Chris Gardner never gives up. Even when the unthinkable happens, he continues pushing forward. He says, "You got a dream … You gotta protect it. People can't do somethin' themselves, they wanna tell you you can't do it. If you want something, go get it. Period."

It's crazy the lengths people can push themselves when in pain, right!?

Failure reminds us why we need to have a growth mindset. It helps us understand that vulnerability is strength. As you begin to develop yourself, trials will doubtlessly appear, and improvement will at times seem impossible. It may feel like you are King Sisyphus in the Greek myth, eternally cursed to roll a massive boulder up a hill only to have it roll back down every time you near the top. Everybody has a giant boulder that we are working with. Sometimes many boulders.

But unlike Sisyphus, once we get our boulders moving, we can reach the top if we just keep pushing. The key is to not let up. Even when things seem to get a little easier, we have to keep working just as hard as when things are difficult. That's the catch. All those little things that help make you successful are so easy to do. But they are so easy not to do also.

You can make a simple decision each and every morning that you are going to be a little better than you were yesterday, despite your circumstances, your history, or your weaknesses. Researchers from the University of North Carolina at Charlotte have been studying trauma and found that a majority of the survivors of trauma report at least one positive outcome, including things like a greater appreciation of life and a greater sense of one's own strength.[5] They are quick to clarify that just because people experience growth does not mean they don't suffer, nor do they claim traumatic events are good. But their research proves that hard things can, indeed, be beneficial for us.

I once worked with an endurance coach named Chris Hauth. In my opinion he is the best in the biz. He worked with me on my mental strength as much as he did on my physical strength. He once said something that has lasted with me for a long time and gets me through hard and low points in my life. He said, "Character is like a photograph; it develops in the darkness." In those dark moments when you are questioning everything, that's where your character,

---

5   Richard G. Tedeschi and Lawrence G. Calhoun, *Trauma & Transformation: Growing in the Aftermath of Suffering* (Thousand Oaks, CA: Sage Publications, 1995).

your tenacity, your desire, your purpose, and your care for who you want to be will display itself.

Mahatma Gandhi taught that there are things that will destroy us: 1) pleasure without conscience, 2) knowledge without character, 3) religion without sacrifice, 4) politics without principle, 5) science without humanity, 6) wealth without work, and 7) business without ethics.[6]

Each of these could be its own book in and of itself, but I hope you will take a moment to consider where your flaws lie and what small, steady steps you can take today to become your best self.

Personal Growth

I have noticed that most of the biggest challenges in my life involve major life choices that I decided without the understanding of their consequences. Going to college, coming back to the family farm, marrying my wife, and becoming a Christian—I took on each of these changes without knowing where they were going to take me. And they all changed the environments I lived in, the people I lived with, and the daily habits and experiences that made up my life.

In the book *Deep Change* by Robert Quinn, this is what he calls "walking naked into the land of uncertainty."[7] The desire to be certain or known is a completely natural human need. Humans are relational. But there are times when we live in the unknown. If we develop the competence to embrace these times rather than trying to shut them down prematurely, the magic of genuine learning, having

---

6   Stephen R. Covey, "Seven Deadly Sins," Gandhi Research Foundation, accessed June 6, 2023, https://www.mkgandhi.org/mgmnt.htm.

7   Robert E. Quinn, *Deep Change: Discovering the Leader Within* (New Jersey: Jossey-Bass, 1996).

a paradigm shift, and achieving a better result than we have in the past can take place.

Entrepreneur, author, and all-around great human, Jesse Itzler said, "I believe in life resumes. Do more. Create memories."[8] A major part of the principle of personal growth is to get out of your comfort zone. Right before he died, my grandfather said, "You need to come back home and work on the farm. I know you don't like getting dirty, but you need to get out of your comfort zone and work with your dad and uncle."

Following that advice was hugely difficult for me, but it was the best thing I ever did. Discomfort often comes from not realizing that there are many other opportunities available to you. Or from seeing those opportunities and believing you can never take advantage of them. Growth demands a new you. Starting before you think you are ready isn't easy, but if you want to change, it is necessary. Waiting for the time to be right to change is like standing on the side of a river and saying, "I'll cross when it's done passing."

Change happens when we recognize that the pain of living in a stagnant, unsatisfying, and familiar place is worse than the discomfort of stepping outside it. Don't let fear be a noose around your neck. Fear of the unknown, uncertainty, and failure are big causes of lack of growth. Uncertainty is the way.

It's important to just take that first step. When you are not moving, you are not learning or building new skills. You are simply existing in time but not evolving through it. Find a goal that inspires you. Carol Dweck suggests in her book *Mindset* that your qualities, confidence, and capabilities are not fixed; they are mobile. They evolve just like you, if you let them.

---

8   Jesse Itzler, *Living with a SEAL: 31 Days Training with the Toughest Man on the Planet* (New York: Center Street, 2016).

When I find that I'm in that stagnant zone, there are a few things that I have learned to try. Here's a short list that might help if you also find you are not progressing the way you wish you could. They are a key part of my "code":

- I show up. I get comfortable being uncomfortable, knowing that the unknown in the uncomfortability is where the growth happens. I always try to value growth over comfort.
- I reflect on my motivations. I get clear on why I want to step outside of my comfort zone.
- I write down a goal. I remind myself every day of that goal. I make sure that that goal will make an impact on me and those around me in a positive light. One of my goals this year was to write this book. I'm not a writer—this is way out of my comfort zone. A goal is not about achievement but about the person you become through it.
- See yourself today and behave as who you want to be tomorrow. Know that you can figure it out and you can make it happen.
- Reframe fear into excitement. Understand that discomfort is the way forward, and there is no other way. I learned this at the age of forty when I decided to take on an Ironman, and I embraced it at the age of fifty when I ruptured my Achilles tendon.
- Take baby steps. Action begets clarity. Keep moving forward, and never give up.
- Have a huge cheer squad. Have a circle of people that will lift you up and not shut you down. Those that will see your enthusiasm and cheer you on.
- Let go of the critics, and hold on to the supporters.

- Don't take yourself too seriously. Laugh at yourself, and know you will make mistakes. What is the meaning of a win if we never learn how to lose?
- Focus on the good stuff. Fertilize your strengths. Celebrate your wins. Enjoy the journey of figuring it out.

None of us is perfect. And that's OK. We can embrace our imperfections and our mistakes to create the type of legacy we want to hand over. If my grandmother had spent her life dwelling on everything that was wrong in her life, it would have had a much, much different result—she would've passed the garbage rather than the legacy. And I am certain the lives of her children, grandchildren, and great-grandchildren would have taken a drearier route as well. The legacy she has passed is built on, first, knowing who we are. Once we know what makes us tick, we can better walk down the path of living and leaving a legacy that matters. We will be on the path to living our own farmer's code.

three

Tilling

FAITH IS TAKING THE FIRST STEP, EVEN WHEN
YOU DON'T SEE THE WHOLE STAIRCASE.

Dr. Martin Luther King, Jr.

The Farmer's Code

Tilling the land can be long and hard work. It can require working twenty-four hours a day to prep a field. The land must be turned and worked to prepare the soil before planting the crops, and it is a process that must continually happen to create a quality seed bed. Tilling means busting up clods and removing rocks, stumps, bits of old trash that will, if left alone, impede the growth of the crop. It is a crucial first step to prepare the soil before any sowing of seeds can begin.

We have to have faith that the tilling we do will create future growth and success for the plant. This work requires a lot of grit, because it is usually done when the early spring weather is volatile.

It requires self-discipline and sacrifice but leads to healthy growth and development, which ultimately creates an incredible legacy. Most importantly it requires a great deal of faith to know that all the effort is for the benefit of a future you cannot yet see.

Never Give Up

Viktor Frankl's perennial bestseller *Man's Search for Meaning* is considered one of the most influential books in America, right up there with Carnegie's *How to Win Friends and Influence People* and Covey's *The 7 Habits of Highly Effective People.*

Most people are aware that Frankl was an up-and-coming psychiatrist in Vienna, Austria, during the Nazi annexation. In the days leading up to World War II, the United States offered him a visa to escape the mounting persecution against Jews of high profile. But he turned down the chance at asylum when he discovered that none of his family would be allowed to join him, a choice that ultimately doomed him to three years living in concentration camps. His father, mother, brother, and pregnant wife all perished, leaving him to pick up the pieces of a shattered life after the camps were liberated in 1945.

A year later he dictated *Ein Psychologe erlebt das Konzentrationslager* (*A Psychologist Experiences the Concentration Camp*) over the course of nine days, later published in English with the title *From Death Camp to Existentialism* and in subsequent editions as *Man's Search for Meaning.* An international bestseller for years, the book chronicles his experiences in some of the most horrific circumstances in history and offers the perspective that life never ceases to have meaning, that we all have a choice in how we choose to react, and that our thoughts, feelings, and actions are not solely a result of our conditions. One of the most famous lines reads, "Those who have a 'why' to live, can bear with almost any 'how.'"[9]

This is all fairly common knowledge and is maintained by the Viktor Frankl Institute that still operates in Vienna. But what most people don't realize is that he was not a prominent psychiatrist after the war, after returning to Vienna and spending many years rebuilding his psychiatry practice. He was considered a secular Jew, especially after he married Eleonore Schwindt, a devout Catholic, and he rarely associated with the Jewish community in any way. By his actions many assumed he had given up on any faith in God.

Virtually everyone in his field was loyal to Sigmund Freud, Alfred Adler, and Carl Jung. His radical beliefs challenged the prevailing view of psychology at the time, and as the lone dissenter in his field, he was taunted and shunned by his peers.

But an interaction with an energetic eighty-five-year-old woman named Marguerite Chajes shed light on a faith he held dear. In preparation for a trip from Brooklyn to Vienna, her rabbi requested she take a message to the famous Mr. Frankl: "Remain strong! Continue your work with complete resolve. Don't give up. Ultimately you will prevail."[10]

As she delivered the message to the apparently apathetic doctor, she noticed tears fill his eyes. After a moment, he explained that he was at the brink of abandoning his life's work and leaving his beloved Vienna due to the pressure from the scholars of his time. This message sent from an inspired and loving rabbi from the other side of the world reinvigorated him. He published *Man's Search for Meaning* shortly

---

9   Viktor Frankl, *Man's Search for Meaning* (Boston: Beacon Press, 2006).

10   Jacob Biderman, "The Rebbe and Viktor Frankl," Chabad .org, accessed June 6, 2023, https://www.chabad.org/therebbe/article_cdo/aid/1201321/jewish/The-Rebbe-and-Viktor-Frankl.htm.

after this interaction and touched the world through his words. This simple reminder that God was aware of him was all he needed to fulfill his divine potential.

In the only authorized biography of his life, his wife describes him as a man of faith, one who never missed a day of prayer for more than fifty years.

Faith and Grit

I believe we all have divine potential, and by whatever name you want to give it, there is a divine force that is aware of us and is guiding our lives. My particular faith is in the Christian version of God, Jesus Christ, and the Holy Spirit. There is a difference between belief in God and faith. To me faith is believing in the power of grace from a high power, but that doesn't have to be the same for everyone. You may have a different version of faith, but I believe it is rare to find someone with absolutely no faith at all. Even they will usually concede that there is a guiding force, a "gut" instinct that should be trusted.

I love adventure. And I love to push myself both physically and mentally. I like to see where the limit is, where I'll actually throw in the towel and quit. But the greatest adventure is following Jesus. Through God I have a better understanding of who I am, while being led by the Holy Spirit. There is nothing more adventurous than that.

I live by the fruit of the Spirit and have trust that faith will cultivate my own great potential. And yours. And everyone else's on earth. We all have rich contributions that we can make to everyone around us and great accomplishments just waiting to be realized.

My sister-in-law Gina stated it beautifully in an interview where she was asked to define faith:

How do you define faith? That's so hard. As a teacher, I've asked my students to do this very thing, and now I feel their pain!

I see faith as a focus on purpose. It is believing your dedication and all your efforts are paying forward to people you love and respect within boundaries. Your faith kind of sets the boundaries, that golden rule.

Faith is also a mirror to me, constantly looking at myself and examining my own focus on purpose. Greg and I are practicing Catholics, and so there's that formality of faith, and we lean on that a lot. But I think what's more important is the focus on believing well in ourselves.

Faith has always been something I could talk to Vivian, my grandmother-in-law, and Mary, my mother-in-law, about. It's a running thread, and it ties us all together.

When things go south (which they do), we lean on it. And when things are great, we give credit. I think we all tend to focus on believing in something bigger.

Knowing that you are being guided and protected by a greater force than yourself cultivates an atmosphere of trust. You have to have strong faith to be in agriculture, because every day is a day of trust. When you put seeds in the ground every year, you trust that they will sprout and eventually grow into something that can care for your whole family. My grandfather took virgin desert dirt and turned it into some of the most productive farm ground in the world. If he hadn't been willing to take that first step of faith, we wouldn't be who we are today.

From that deep and abiding principle, our family has learned to trust in each other. We have different jobs and responsibilities that are widely different from each other, but despite that, we have faith that each one of us will do good for the good of the family. Everyone functions at a high level because of this trust.

My wife, Jenn, recently started working for a nonprofit organization in our hometown called Bakersfield Angel's, and I love that she works there. This organization walks alongside children, youth, and families in the foster care community by offering support through intentional giving, relationship building, and mentorship. The work they are doing is changing the outcomes of youth in foster care. Young adults are graduating from high school, going to college, and getting jobs rather than finding homelessness and prison as their path through life.

Jenn is the director of the mentoring program, but true to her agricultural roots, she works farmers hours. It is not easy to be on call twenty-four hours a day, seven days a week, but it is easy for her to maintain grit and resilience as she is working for something bigger than herself. When you know other people are counting on you, there is always an extra reserve of energy.

There are times when we struggle or don't feel comfortable with something. We all know that we can safely come forward, because we trust that no matter what, we will be treated with respect and love. I've got faith I can always lean on my brother and cousin and that they will always be there for me. Our best interests and the best interests of the family are always the number one consideration. Faith and trust do not leave much space for ego and doubt; they provide space for potential to work its magic.

Do Hard Things

The term "idiot" is an ugly one. But the word is derived from the ancient Greek word "idios," which essentially means that if you don't take interest in life beyond yourself, you are an "idiot." What the ancient Greeks are saying is that if you don't create something that lasts and are concerned for the betterment of future generations, it is "idios."

So how do you not live a life of "idios"?

Initiative activates you. You have to find that ability to take initiative to get what you want. Determination and grit are also part of faithfulness. I recently did an endurance event called 29029 Everesting. It took place in Whistler, Canada. The event is one where you hike up to the peak of Whistler, 3.9 miles with a 3,900-foot elevation gain. You must hike up eight times in thirty-six hours, essentially climbing the same elevation as Mount Everest, all for the glory of a red hat—if you accomplish Everest.

> FAITH AND TRUST DO NOT LEAVE MUCH SPACE FOR EGO AND DOUBT; THEY PROVIDE SPACE FOR POTENTIAL TO WORK ITS MAGIC.

It is one of the most challenging events I have ever done, and I've done some crazy things—like Ironman. What you must know about me is that I'm a big guy, six feet three inches, 240 pounds. There is a Clydesdale category in many endurance events for men over two hundred pounds. I'm a super Clydesdale. Point being I'm not your typical endurance athlete.

It is really easy in life to tell yourself to stay in your lane. "Mike, you are way too big to do crazy endurance events! Stay in your lane and just cheer the little guys on."

To that I say, "No way."

Endurance events certainly wouldn't be "my lane," especially when you look at me. But I do them anyway. I do them to get uncomfortable, so that I can find out who I am on the other side. Who will I become after I cover thirty-two miles and 29,029 feet of elevation gain in thirty-six hours?

There was a point during the Everest event where I lost my phone. It was dark, cold, and raining, and my legs wouldn't move. I couldn't call my wife for motivation. It was just me and the mountain. I was tired and feeling sorry for myself because at that point I had forgotten why I was there. Mike Tyson said, "Everyone has a plan until they get punched in the face." The mountain just punched me in the face. I was telling myself things like, "What the hell are you doing? This is crazy. You're the biggest guy out here. You don't have what it takes. There is no way you will finish." I was caught up in a constant stream of doubt.

Thankfully, it was momentary. I finally saw life beyond my doubts. One of the coaches caught me to ask how I was doing. She didn't really need an answer as her headlamp shined in my eyes, because she saw it. She asked me, "Why are you here?"

I said, "Because I like to do hard things."

She said, "Well, you've clearly found hard. Shake it off and remind yourself of your determination and grit. Just put one foot in front of the other. Don't stop until you put on that red hat."

For the remainder of the night, I put one foot in front of the other and reminded myself that I am strong, and I love hard things. I had faith that my training and the community of people on that mountain would get me across the finish line. As night turned into day, I found a new energy. After thirty hours on the mountain, I made that final ascent, and I got my red hat.

As I told this story to a friend afterward, he said, "Mike, you could've just bought yourself a red hat and avoided all the pain." But it's not about the red hat. It's about what the red hat represents—faith, grit, and determination.

To have faith, I don't worry. I find comfort in the unknown. It is easy for me to harbor an incessant need to try to seize control of my life, because uncertainty and imperfection are scary things. But this is also the fertile ground where I find a dependence on God. I trust that this is a dependence that will lead to a better end than I could ever design on my own.

Listening to feelings from your heart, mind, and soul requires faith. Many of these feelings are formed from past lessons and experiences. Value those instincts because they will help you create an environment that allows those close to you to explore their own inner voices. Passing on that kind of faith can lead to legacies that are eternal.

To live your own farmer's code, you must have enough grit to persist faithfully in the face of failure. Your code must include believing in yourself.

four

Maintaining

IT'S NOT THE MOUNTAIN WE CONQUER BUT OURSELVES.

Sir Edmund Hillary

The Farmer's Code

It takes a lot of horsepower to operate a farm. Today, that means tractors, both big and small. Our tractors work year-round and must always be ready on short notice. We must always be working on and maintaining our equipment so that when it is needed, it can be trusted to get the job done. The tractor on the cover of this book is the first tractor my grandfather purchased in 1945. We still have it today.

Just as we must maintain our tractors to ensure they are in good working condition to perform their tasks effectively, we must also maintain a positive attitude and make good decisions in order to achieve our goals. Mental and emotional maintenance is one of the keys to a successful life. A great attitude and good decisions are a large piece of the "farmer's code."

Wake-Up Call

As the twig is bent, so the tree is inclined, according to the proverbial saying. Each and every action you take shapes you into the human you will ultimately become. This means that every day you make a choice from the moment you wake up: thrive or survive.

There was a point in my life that I was one of those people who subconsciously chose "survive" over "thrive" every day. I got up. Ate breakfast. Went to work. Came home. Went to bed.

In short, I survived. That was all. I was making choices that weren't filling my cup but rather making me feel empty. I thought that being a good dad and being "all in" on my family and my work meant I had to be "all out" on myself. But what this did was drive me to a place where I was unproductive for anyone and even more destructive with myself.

As I mentioned in chapter 1, I wasn't sure that I really wanted to come back to the family business, but I honored my grandfather's request. While today I know that besides marrying my wife, coming back home was one of the smartest decisions I ever made, it took a few years for me to get to that place. During that time we had our first baby, and I was working many, many hours on the ranch, with no "me time." When I took that "me time," it usually entailed me doing things that I wasn't proud of.

It all caught up with me one night after playing golf and having way too much to drink. I proceeded to drive home and was luckily stopped and taken to jail for a DUI. That moment changed my life forever. It was the first time I was in any significant amount of trouble, and it was the first time I had ever gone to jail. I was scared and ashamed.

As I sat in the drunk tank that night, I had a lot to think about. The cell was crowded, people passed out on the floor, one guy puking on my shoes. It was miserable. I was determined to not fall asleep that night.

Well, one hour turned into another, which turned into eight. I decided maybe I could try to doze with one eye open. All of a sudden, I was in this dream. It was foggy outside, and the presence of someone whom I now know to be Jesus Christ was standing in front of me. My grandfather stood next to him, and my whole family stood there, even generations past that I didn't know.

My grandfather spoke, saying, "Michael, if you are going to lead this family, you need to change your ways. Clean up your act. Be the leader we know you are. We love you and know you are capable of so much more."

And with that I was completely jolted out of that dream. One of the drunks next to me saw me jerk out of my sleep and sit straight up. I'm sure my eyes were bugged out of my head with a complete look of shock and wonder on my face. He said, "Man, I'm not sure what you drank to get in here last night, but whatever it was I want two when I get out of this place. I've never seen such determined eyes on someone when they wake up."

That day, waking up on that hard bench in that vomit-infested jail cell, I decided I couldn't live another minute the way I was living. I was choosing to survive and not to thrive.

As unhealthy as I was, I made a choice that I wanted to thrive and that going all in on everything was not only possible but necessary. I needed balance in my life, so I started working on me.

Every Decision Counts

The principle of the compound effect was a logical place to begin (made famous by Darren Hardy's book by the same name, *The Compound Effect*). If you are unfamiliar with this principle, I'll do my best to explain it.

A stranger approaches you and a friend and says, "I have $3 million in cash to give away. I will give that entire amount to one of you. To the other, I will give a magic penny that doubles in value every day for one month."

Which would you pick?

Let's say you give the $3 million to your friend and take the penny for yourself, even though it seems a little absurd to give that much money away. Who takes a penny over millions in cash?

By the end of the week, your friend is doing what most people do with sudden wealth—spending it on luxury and adventure.

You, on the other hand, have been watching despondently as your penny becomes two pennies, then four pennies, then eight.

Twenty days in, and you look and see that you have $5,000. Not bad. It's not $3 million, but your friend has already blown through a sizable chunk of that, so things aren't as bleak as they were.

At twenty-nine days, you have $2.7 million, so you're almost caught up to your friend. And you smile thinking that there are still two days left.

The next day brings you to $5.3 million, and then, on the very last day, you see that your decision to take the penny was genius. You wake up to $10,737,418.24.

With each and every choice you make, every single day, you are either adding to your inherent value or taking away from it. Every morning brings you opportunities to invest in yourself in a way that compounds over time. When you choose to learn something new, exercise your body, strengthen your relationships, or take countless other self-improving actions, you're essentially choosing the magic penny.

There are so many ridiculous messages out there claiming you can get rich working only four hours a week, lose weight with a pill, or become popular with a pair of shoes. It's all nonsense. If you want to get rich, lose weight, become influential, or achieve intergalactic domination, you have to do the work. There are no shortcuts. As Jeff Olson says in his book *The Slight Edge*, "There are two kinds of habits: those that serve you, and those that don't."[11]

In Angela Duckworth's book *Grit*, she found that people with extraordinary willpower actually use less of it than the rest of us. Meaning the more willpower you have, the less you use. The reason for that is people with high self-control know that it's toxic to push yourself to do something you don't want to do. So instead they try to rearrange the situations they are in so they don't have to rely on as much willpower. It comes down to consistency and habits. You don't have to motivate yourself to brush your teeth, do you? No. Because you have been doing it consistently your whole life. People who jog every day will tell you that they don't love to run. It's just something that they get up and do every morning.

This might sound a little ridiculous, but the principle is this: you do things because you do them. Simple as that.

Attitude Counts

If you have never stopped to consider what fruits your actions bear, this might be a good time to stop and take stock. Brushing your teeth

---

11   Jeff Olson, *The Slight Edge* (Austin: Greenleaf Book Group Press, 2013).

equals healthy oral hygiene. Positive fruit. Smoking equals decreased health and financial burden. Negative fruit. Signing up for a class equals improved professional and/or personal skills. Positive fruit. Surfing the internet aimlessly for hours equals wasted time and potentially missed opportunities. Negative fruit.

Additionally, your attitude points you in the direction of depletion or improvement with each decision. You can achieve a hundred doctorate degrees, but without the right attitude, it won't do you or anyone else around you much good.

Every day my prayer is to step into the day with a smile on my face, to be heart led in everything I do. This sometimes means cutting ties and distancing myself from those who have a bad attitude. Bad attitudes are like a wave in the ocean. They will swallow you up and tow you under.

> BAD ATTITUDES ARE LIKE A WAVE IN THE OCEAN. THEY WILL SWALLOW YOU UP AND TOW YOU UNDER.

We are all responsible for our own attitudes. In every situation, your attitude matters. As mentioned in the last chapter, our circumstances do not need to dictate our emotions. We are all masters of our own fate.

What sets my family apart, in my opinion, is that nobody plays the victim. We are all owners of our own mindset, and this is non-negotiable. Not that there weren't plenty of opportunities for people to legitimately feel as though they were a victim.

My dad always encouraged my brother and me to make the best of every situation, no matter what it was. He grew up on a small farm with an alcoholic father who was satisfied with what he had, even though he only owned a fraction of the land he farmed. My dad's father dropped out of high school by the time he was thirteen and was riding freight trains to harvest grain in Kansas during the Depression. He settled on the farm after WWII and never really tried to grow or improve.

My father, fearing he would be drafted, joined the navy reserves after attending community college for two-and-a-half years. He quickly discovered the navy wasn't for him, so he volunteered for the draft to get out of the navy. Volunteering for the draft during the Vietnam War may seem crazy, but he figured it was either six years of reserves with two years of active duty with the navy or only two years active duty with the draft. He figured the shorter the better.

When inducted into the army, he was sent to Fort Lewis, in Washington State, where he spent five months in training. Among other things, he was given a questionnaire the soldiers affectionately called the "dream sheet," where he could list what job he wanted and where he might like to be stationed in the army. His "dream sheet" listed "finance clerk and Italy."

Five months later he was an infantryman in Vietnam carrying an M60 machine gun. I know, that's an awful long way from Italy.

I was named after his best friend, Michael, from his time in Fort Lewis. They were in the same squad through infantry training and spent the weekends visiting Michael's family in Portland. They stayed close after they were deployed until Michael was killed in action, along with over fifty-eight thousand Americans.

You'd expect my dad to be negative about this chapter in his life. When soldiers returned home, people spit on them and called them baby killers. But Dad said, "I was a big guy, and I didn't put up with much, but a lot of guys were treated harshly. You can protest war, but you don't protest the warriors. We were just doing our duty to our nation."

When he came back, he married my mother and finished college, and they started a family.

When he reflected on experiences in the war, he said, "I didn't have a bad experience. I actually had a lot of great memories from it. Typically with things like that, you're aware of the bad things that happen, but it's the good things that you remember."

He had every reason in the world to feel like a victim, but he didn't. Ever. He has always had a talent for keeping a positive perspective and choosing his attitude, no matter what circumstances he is in.

I know that sometimes it is tempting to think, "But if only…"

If only I were smarter.
If only I were better looking.
If only I had more money.
If only I were talented.

These are all excuses. You don't have to have a lot of talent to get ahead in life. I certainly don't, but I do choose to focus each day on having a great attitude, surrounding myself with loyal people, choosing to encourage and bring the best out in those around me, smiling bigger, showing up more, working harder, reading more than the average person, and listening to more podcasts than the average person, because I'm determined to let my attitude drive my outcomes.

I am not better than anyone else. Far from it! I have been lucky enough to learn that self-discipline leads to reaching goals. My grandfather showed this as a flight instructor in teaching hundreds of WWII pilots how to fly over the fields of California before being deployed. And my family has shown this by doing the work daily in farming that brings in the yields to support us.

The people who are the most successful in life don't waste time proving that they can do whatever it is they do. No. They just do the things they need to do routinely, and then they go beyond their basic abilities to find a path to success that is unique to their specific circumstances.

A Few Suggestions

If you are wanting to achieve bigger and better goals for yourself, I have a couple of suggestions that can help you compound your penny, so to speak.

1. Find time for solitude. This can mean meditation, introspection, or prayer. Doing this will help you better know yourself. Solitude can also mean friendship. This may not sound like solitude, as friendship can often mean being with many other people. But I'm talking about a deep friendship, with intimate conversation. One where you listen as much as you speak. This is a form of introspection. Find someone you can trust where you can unpack your soul. You need this to learn more about yourself and help you develop independent thoughts. Solitude is important. Imagine where America would be without the solitude of Thomas Jefferson, John Adams, Alexander Hamilton, or James Madison. To put it plainly, there would be no America.

2. Read books! Not just tweets, social media, or even old-fashioned media. Books are old. A person who writes a book has thought about their subject carefully. The book is a result of their solitude and their attempt to think for themself. When you read a book and you put it down, it can continue to live with you, and you will think about what you are reading. Tweets and social media bombard you with other people's thoughts and other people's realities. It is impossible to hear

your own voice when you are bombarded in this manner. Books give you the time to read, learn, and reflect. They allow you to develop your own original thoughts. An African proverb tells us that when an old person dies, a library burns to the ground. Build the library in your head!

3. Set goals! Don't just make New Year's resolutions that fade away before the end of January. Put your goals in writing. As my friend and author Jack Daly says, "If your goals are not in writing, they are dreams. Dreams don't often come true, but goals in writing do."[12] Once you have your goals in writing, track them. When you track your progress to your goals, you inherently hold yourself accountable. But don't just count on yourself; get an accountability partner to keep you on track. When you have a cheerleader on your side, it is much easier to accomplish your goals when the task gets tedious.

4. Establish a daily routine. Start with things that are nonnegotiable. Things that fill up your cup. For me, if I can hit these daily "vitamins," I know that my day will be nourished. First, I try to wake up early. There is so much peace to find before the sun comes up. Then I hydrate. It wakes up my body and kick-starts the rest of the day. Next, I move—some sort of exercise outside while watching the sun rise brings so much nourishment to my soul. Then quiet time with my dog. This is pure relaxation for me. After that it is some sort of cold-water therapy, be it a cold shower, a swim in the ocean, or a cold plunge. It is said that cold-water therapy can boost the immune system, improve circulation, reduce inflammation, boost energy, and improve sleep. But I enjoy

---

12   Jack Daly, "Turning Goals into Reality," jackdalysales.com, accessed June 6, 2023, https://jackdalysales.com/turning-goals-into-reality/.

the mental challenge and the resilience that is learned by subjecting myself to the cold. Last, tell someone you love them. Get physical while doing it via a hug or a kiss. The endorphins set the day for the perfect launch.

Everyone is born with potential. But it's what you do with it that separates the survivors from the thrivers. Don't just white-knuckle life or be resigned to barely getting by. To live the farmer's code, you must thrive by living and thinking abundantly. Don't waste your gift! Live the code.

five

Replenishing

The Farmer's Code

My grandfather always said, "Feed the land to feed the people to feed our family." I believe there is no greater steward of the land than a farmer. Wise farmers will continually care for the land by regenerating and replenishing it with macro and micronutrients through the organic matter that is crucial to the farmers' existence.

Just as we replenish the soil, we can replenish the lives of those around us by adding humor and positivity. Touching the lives of others in this way is a great way to leave and have a rememberable legacy.

Thick Skin

The human body is miraculous in its design, in large part because of our remarkable protection system—our skin. Skin is probably the most amazing and least appreciated organ we have. If we are cut, we heal. If we fall and scrape our knee, it scabs over. If we are burned, we grow new skin. Our skin can be put through incredible stresses and still shield us from harm.

We have around seventeen thousand nerve receptors in one hand, concentrated mostly in the fingers, which help us detect a bump as small as 0.2 millimeters. That's the thickness of two eyelashes. And they become even more reactive when they are in motion.

The same can be said for our emotional "skin." Having a "thick skin" prevents us from taking offense to others too easily. We can give the benefit of the doubt and laugh it off. We let petty slights go without it affecting us. In essence we're easier to get along with.

Sure, life is going to knock us around, and we can develop emotional calluses that protect us from listening to critics and complainers and from allowing the wrong people power in our lives. When we are less easily hurt, we are less likely to get sidetracked in trying to defend ourselves or shutting down. We don't have to invest our energy in things that are of little importance.

People who have a thin emotional skin tend to focus on protecting themselves and everyone around them, which is an impossible and often counterproductive effort, diluting their ability to focus on real priorities. They spend their time in futile attempts to prevent imagined future offenses.

My uncle Rick said, "You don't have anything if you don't have a sense of humor." That's what creates patience in a family. So we can kind of laugh at each other and enjoy our own weaknesses, our own faults, and our strengths. Everybody's got big enough shoulders where they can take a little criticism. But you have to be able to laugh and say, "Yeah, you're right. I have that as a weakness."

Our emotional skin allows us to be touched by generations before us. We don't have to have such thick skin that we are completely hardened. There is a fine line between protecting yourself and shutting things out. Don't let calluses make you callous.

Having a thick skin doesn't mean we have to be abrasive. When it comes to building relationships, having a gentle touch is key. Doesn't the world have enough people who are tough, coarse, rude, greedy, vain, and confrontational? We need more people who are tender, kind, good, gracious, and refined. We have enough people who seek fame and fortune. We need more compassion and dignity. We need more gentle touches.

> DOESN'T THE WORLD HAVE ENOUGH PEOPLE WHO ARE TOUGH, COARSE, RUDE, GREEDY, VAIN, AND CONFRONTATIONAL? WE NEED MORE PEOPLE WHO ARE TENDER, KIND, GOOD, GRACIOUS, AND REFINED.

Humor

Where do they make average things? At the Satisfactory!

Did you smile there, even on the inside? Humor is an emotional pressure-relief valve. We use it to defuse tense situations, to give us perspective, and to provide a safe outlet for emotions that threaten to overwhelm. Who doesn't love a good joke? Comedy has come a long way from Groucho Marx and the Three Stooges. Whether it is the famous observational Jerry Seinfeld quips or the deadpan Steven Wright one-liners, humor is one of my favorite aspects of being a human being.

My cousin Greg shares a story about how humor was both inappropriate and fully appropriate in his life.

One time when I was in high school, my grandpa had to borrow my truck, as his truck needed service. He knew my truck was at our house because I was working in the fields, driving a tractor. The problem was that I had bought an Andrew Dice Clay comedy CD and had it playing when I last shut off my truck. When he got in the truck, it was playing on the louder side. He couldn't figure out how to turn it off either. So, needless to say, he got angrier from every off-color joke that Mr. Dice Clay told after he started it up. He drove straight out to the tractor I was on, and I could see the dust plume coming from behind the truck as he sped toward me.

At the time I had no idea what was going on, so I was wondering why my truck was coming toward me at such an alarming rate. He drove right out into the field. Even though I was about midway in one of my passes, he couldn't wait for me to get to the end of the field. I shut off the tractor as he got out of the truck, and I could tell he was upset because his cheeks were bright red, like they always got when he was angry. I could hear the comedy routine coming from my truck as he stormed toward me.

He started yelling things like, "Is this the kind of trash your generation listens to? Is this what makes you tick?"

It was not funny at the time, but reflecting upon this story with my family later, we all got a kick out of it. We knew that this was just comedy, and we could all laugh at it. But my grandfather was very passionate and had a short fuse, and we all knew it.

He interpreted it that maybe our generation was going down the wrong path. I know he was worried in that moment that maybe I was listening to pagan comedy, and maybe it would make my path in life stray from the path he had envisioned for me. All turned out well, and, looking back, it was a pretty funny moment involving my grandfather's temper and him being worried about me and our whole generation.

Don't Take Yourself Too Seriously

Having a sense of humor is one of the constants of our family. We laugh often. We laugh loud. And we laugh together. As part of the research for this book, I interviewed fifteen people, mostly my close relatives. Every single person commented on the way we are able to laugh at ourselves and at each other without getting upset.

We have a few favorite stories that we tell when we get in the right mood that teach the next generation the value of not taking ourselves too seriously.

A story that we love to tell the grandkids happened when I was in my early teens. My brother, Jeff, shares his memory of what happened.

One of my favorite stories about Grandpa was at a house they had up in Sun River, Oregon. I remember us four grandkids up with them, so it was just the six of us. Grandpa was cooking dinner one night, barbecuing steaks. And we went out for a bike ride out on the bike path while they cooked. Greg and I were racing back home, and we got to the house first. We saw all this smoke coming up out of the garage, and we were sure that the house was on fire. We rode right into the garage, jumped off our bikes, and grabbed the fire extinguisher, spraying down the barbecue to put out the fire.

It was literally just a charcoal fire, a normal barbecue fire on those steaks. The steaks were probably burned, I really don't know, but they definitely had the fire extinguisher stuff all over them. Grandpa came back, and oh he was hot. He was so mad that we ruined the steaks over a barbecue fire.

He went into the garage, took them all off the grill, went into the kitchen, scraped all the white stuff into the sink, and made us eat them for dinner. Grandma was yelling at him and saying, "We can't eat this!"

He was like, "Damn it. We're eating these things. Those kids ruined it. We spent good money on this, so we're eating them."

And we were so proud too. We thought we saved the house. He didn't agree.

I like to look back at that, and while it probably wasn't as funny at the time, it's sure funny now. It's definitely one of our cherished memories.

We all laughed about that for years, even my grandpa.

But my favorite story is about GG. We were all together for Christmas dinner a number of years ago, and she had agreed to bless the food. She gave a lovely prayer, but then out of the blue, right at the end, she added, "Jesus, please don't let any of my grandchildren or great-grandchildren get a tattoo." She went on and on and on about them and then finally said, "Amen."

It struck us as such a funny thing to pray for. We all laughed about it and started eating. Since then, it has become infamous. We all call it "the tattoo prayer." When my daughter brought home a boyfriend who has a few tattoos, she didn't go straight into the living room to greet GG. Instead, she pulled him aside and had him pull his long sleeves down so his tattoos were hidden.

We asked GG about the tattoo prayer, and she explained that her brother, who she loved dearly, was in the army in Honolulu during World War II. He and a bunch of his buddies got drunk, and they all went down to the tattoo parlor, and he got one on his arm. He's hated it his whole life. She said, "You think you have this wonderful tattoo, but over time, they just slide and melt. They are awful. I wanted to get it across to the kids that tattoos stay with you forever. That prayer was a good opportunity to get them all at once. I figured they had to listen if it was in the prayer, because nobody else was talking. It was just us and God!"

The Christmas after the tattoo prayer, my sister-in-law Gina went and got a bunch of those temporary tattoos made up of GG's face. She had all the kids put tattoos on their arms and on their chests. When GG saw them, she was delighted. We put them all over her, too, and she loved it.

When she is asked if her prayer worked, if any of her family had tattoos, she gets a twinkle in her eye and says, "They'd better not."

At a sassy one hundred years old, GG certainly can dish out as much as she takes. When everyone is leaving a family get-together and saying their I love yous to her, she'll say something like, "Oh my! To what do I owe the honor of such attention?"

My father will tease her by saying something like, "It's just because you're old and out of shape, so we worry about you."

She grins and fires back, "What did you say, old man?"

Then he'll say something like, "You're just lucky I bred looks and smarts into your family."

And she'll finish with, "You're just lucky we took you in."

GG doesn't miss a beat. My mom says it helps to have a thick skin and maybe a bit of a sour mouth to make it in this family.

The quietest person in our family is my brother-in-law Joe. I think he summed it up perfectly. "We're serious about business, but most of us don't take ourselves too seriously. We can make fun of each other. We can make fun of ourselves, and we all get together every holiday and laugh. Sometimes it gets pretty loud and crude, but we all have a good time with it."

Touching

President Ronald Reagan said in his farewell address to the nation that "All great change in America begins at the dinner table." There is nothing more special than when our family gathers around the dinner table. All twenty-two of us, four generations deep. There is a lot of laughter, a lot of banter, and a lot of unconditional love. The fingerprints left on each family member are prints that last a lifetime.

Jesus Christ spent a lot of time around the dinner table. Many of his most frequently quoted messages and standout stories happened while breaking bread with others. When strangers eat together, they have the chance to become friends. When friends share a meal together, they have the opportunity to touch each other's lives.

While diversity, equity, and inclusion are big buzz words in the world today, there was no one more inclusive than Jesus. During his time on earth, he was a friend to everyone. If you look closely at the company the Savior usually kept around the table, it was a remarkably diverse group. He shared meals with outcasts. He spent time with the self-righteous religious elite. He cared for people who had broken every rule and were seen as unclean. He dined at the tables of the wealthy men whose riches were won with lies and corruption. Some of those men gave up comfortable lifestyles to follow him. He crossed racial boundaries to the shock of many around him. He invited everyone to the table.

In Romans 2:11 KJV, we read, "There is no respect of persons with God," meaning he does not value one life over another. And yet we do that so often with each other. We have created classes, cliques, groups, and titles that single some out while leaving others behind. Our tendency to "otherize" those who are not exactly like us has created deep rifts in our society. Even something as precious as faith has been weaponized.

For example, the name of Jesus has been used in many ways to harm and divide. But if you really understood how he lived, you would understand how contrary that really is. Jesus was not exclusive. He was radically inclusive, and he touched (and continues to touch) many lives. Jesus saw people as individuals with agency, not as victims of social constructs or helpless artifacts of history. What could our world look like today if strangers became friends over the dinner table?

We all know that no two fingerprints are alike. The skin on our fingertips is wrinkled in loops and whorls and has been used for identification as far back as 1700s BC with the Babylonian king, Hammurabi. In this respect our skin does more than protect us. It also shapes our identity.

My girls were avid readers when they were young, and one of their favorite authors was Judy Blume. She once said, "Our fingerprints don't fade from the lives we touch." Live your legacy now, with humor, thick skin, and a willingness to leave fingerprints of love on every life you touch. This is how we replenish the "soil" of our legacy. This is a key piece to the farmer's code.

LD A POSITIVE, PERMANENT *legacy* OUGH DELIBERATE, *daily choices.*

PART 2

Establish Loving Relationships (Us)

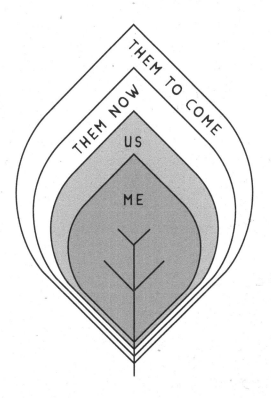

LOVE IS OUR TRUE DESTINY. WE DO NOT FIND THE MEANING
OF LIFE BY OURSELVES ALONE—WE FIND IT WITH ANOTHER.

Thomas Merton

six

Tending

USE YOUR VOICE FOR KINDNESS, YOUR EARS FOR EMPATHY, YOUR HANDS FOR HELPING OTHERS, YOUR MIND FOR TRUTH, AND YOUR HEART FOR COMPASSIONATE LOVE.

Anonymous

The Farmer's Code

Mother Nature can be a beast for any farmer. She dishes out hurricanes, tornadoes, snow, ice, floods, and earthquakes. She also provides rain, nourishing breezes that pollinate, and fresh water. Sure, sometimes we don't like what she does, but without her we wouldn't be able to feed and clothe the world.

Conversely, we have the ability to harm Mother Nature by the way we interact with the soil, the water, and the air. Farmers know that our actions have consequences. Here in America we had to learn this the hard way during the catastrophic Dust Bowl of the 1930s, an event that impacted everyone in the nation for generations, even still today. The agricultural world was called to repentance. The Soil Conservation Service (now the Natural Resources Conservation Service) was founded on the tenet that "Land must be nurtured; not plundered and wasted," as chief Hugh Hammond Bennett put it.[13] Tending is the act of taking care of something or someone. Farmers are constantly tending to the soil, to the animals, and to the crops in order to produce a successful harvest.

If you think about Mother Nature as the ecosystem we live in, you can think about your relationships with others as the ecosystem you live in. Just as farmers recognize the delicate balance of nature and tend to it, we each should also recognize the importance of maintaining balance and harmony in our relationships and interactions with others. Tending requires nurturing, supporting, loving, and forgiving to build healthy, legacy-filled relationships.

Love Is the Fruit of Faith

As I write this book, I am lucky enough to be the chair of the California Agricultural Leadership Foundation, which runs a seventeen-month intensive, transformational leadership development program for those that have the propensity to lead in California agriculture. The focus of the program is learning to lead from the inside out. A number of years ago, I went through the program, as did my uncle Rick and cousin Greg, and we all found it to be a huge part of our self-development journeys. The experience we gained through this

---

13   Mike Lessiter, "10 Maxims from H.H. Bennett, 'Father of Soil Conservation,'" No-Till Farmer, accessed June 6, 2023, https://www.no-tillfarmer.com/articles/11034-10-maxims-from-hh-bennett-father-of-soil conservation#:~:text=Land%20must%20be%20nurtured%3B%20not,also%20moral%20support%20and%20encouragement.%E2%80%9D

program has turned out to be an important piece of the puzzle to our family legacy.

Part of the leadership program is an intensive international travel experience that focuses on learning and leading from experiences beyond our immediate community. A prominent member of Class 25, Richard Peterson has been an integral part of California agriculture for many years. His international trip was to India, where they had the opportunity to meet and serve with Mother Teresa.

Mother Teresa was famous for her service to the most wretched and shunned in the streets of Calcutta. When asked why she would touch these "untouchables," she would often remind people that that person was just Jesus in one of his many distressing disguises.

After working alongside her, Richard Peterson said, "During my career, I promoted fruits of all types, but Mother Teresa introduced our class to the concept of spiritual fruit. She said the fruit of silence is prayer. The fruit of prayer is faith. The fruit of faith is love. The fruit of love is service. The fruit of service is peace. This led me to expand my outreach with a focus on leadership positions in my church and in nonprofits."

Years later Richard was given a Profiles in Leadership award from the California Ag Leadership Foundation for his powerful and consistent service to nonprofits focused on reaching disadvantaged communities throughout the state. Do you see how the fruits of love can be contagious? One cannot leave a legacy until one understands this principle.

What Does It Mean to Be Heart Forward?

Leaving a legacy starts in the heart. When you lead with love, you treat everyone as a human and not an object. When you do so, you are subconsciously choosing to inspire.

We often see fellow humans as objects. We see a title, a label, a habit, an addiction, clothing, cars, online presence … the list goes on. Anything but the actual human being behind all of those things. When we don't allow ourselves to recognize what makes people people, the way we treat others changes. We act/react in ways we never would with close friends and family. Lines are drawn in the sand, and battles begin.

The choice of seeing everyone's humanity must be intentional and has to be done daily. Let's say you see a person experiencing home-lessness walking down the street. Do you think to yourself, "That man is somebody's son. He is probably somebody's brother, husband, and maybe even father. Someone out there loves that man the same way I love my father and my son"?

Or do you drive by, barely recognizing that he is there at all?

In 2017 I read *The Heart-Led Leader* by Tommy Spaulding. It inspired me to think and lead more with my heart. I decided to hold myself accountable to truly being heart led and wanted a way to remind myself how all of my actions had consequences. I wanted to develop an awareness that would become a standard to live by.

So, I bought two fishbowls. The life expectancy of a man of my demographics is around eighty-eight years, so I took one fishbowl and put 1,792 marbles in it, representing the number of weeks I might have left on earth if I live the average life expectancy. At the end of each week, I ask myself this question: Did you live a heart-led week and inspire someone?

By my own standard, if the answer is yes, I move one marble from the full fishbowl to the heart-led bowl. If it is no, I throw that marble away. It is a great way to keep myself in the present and a reminder to always lead with the heart with intent to inspire. It's not about doing something good for charity. It's about how I make others feel. Do I make them feel like their life was better (maybe for even a few minutes) because of their interaction with me?

Love Unconditionally!

I was at a dinner party one night, and the topic of conversation turned to love. A friend at the party said something that has lingered with me. He said love is the ability to accept another exactly as they are at any time. This means showing love for another person without considering how it will benefit you or what you will get in return.

This is hard. But once we surrender to God's unconditional love for us, we can understand how easy this can be. Unconditional love does not mean that God loves everything we do. Rather, his love is so intense that he loves the sinner, not the sin. This is one of the reasons our family has been able to stay in business for four generations now. We love one another for who the other person is, not for their successes or failures.

> WE LOVE ONE ANOTHER FOR WHO THE OTHER PERSON IS, NOT FOR THEIR SUCCESSES OR FAILURES.

My wife, Jenn, shared her thoughts on being a part of this family:

> *We all know we need to look at the bigger picture. The bigger picture is that we're family. We love each other. And yes, we all*

> *have differing opinions about things and often push one another's*
> *buttons, but none of us holds on so tightly that it causes bonds to*
> *sever. There's a mutual respect there. Each one of us has our own*
> *interests and passions, and we show up for one another. I asked*
> *the family to come to a fundraiser for my organization, and we*
> *filled a whole table. They all showed up to support me ... with*
> *their presence and their pocketbooks. That's just how this family is.*

Singer Lionel Richie said, "I think the whole world is dying to hear someone say, 'I love you.' I think that if I can leave the legacy of love and passion in the world, then I think I've done my job in a world that's getting colder and colder by the day."[14] While this may seem somewhat pessimistic in tone, I feel like he's touching on a nerve that we all feel.

When we show our love to those around us, we are able to build a deeper connection and have a more lasting impact on them. We show love through acts of service and by having empathy, as I have discussed in earlier chapters. Everybody has some sort of empathy; it is inherently human. God made us in His image, which means we were made to love. I recognize that empathy is easier for some people than others, but everyone has the capacity to feel it to some degree.

Forgiveness

Forgiveness is a key element of love. Nowhere in the Bible does it talk about forgiveness as a feeling. It talks about forgiveness as a choice and as a decision. Your emotions will eventually follow your decisions. I've traveled to Algeria on a number of occasions for business. The

---

14   Lionel Richie, Quote, BrainyQuote, accessed June 6, 2023, https://www.brainyquote. com/quotes/lionel_richie_508918.

national identity of Algeria is based on a combination of Berber and Arab cultures, and the strong influence of Islam creates a sense of identity that extends beyond national boundaries to include other Arab nations. The Algerian people are some of the most hospitable and generous people I know. Their Islamic foundations provide a consistent emphasis on forgiveness during Ramadan, the month of forgiveness and mercy. I think it is such a beautiful practice to take a full month every year to specifically focus on how we can forgive others and earn the forgiveness of those we have wronged.

It's not easy. Forgiveness is looking at what was done for me, not what was done to me. When you forgive, you let go of the pain. You let go of the garbage that can no longer be passed to the next generation. But if you don't forgive, you hold on to that anger, and it will continually come out. Anger will only weaken you. The longer you hold on to garbage, the more it stinks. Let it go!

E:60 is a sports news and investigative journalism program that airs on ESPN. It is one of my favorite shows, as it features in-depth stories and reports on various sports-related topics. The program's focus is on telling compelling stories and uncovering unique angles that go beyond the scores and highlights of the games. *E:60* also features interviews with players, coaches, and other figures in the sports world as well as commentary and analysis from sports journalists and experts.

On August 4, 2015, ESPN aired an episode[15] of the show that delivered one of the most powerful messages of love and forgiveness that I had ever seen. It was an interview with Chris Singleton, who at the time was a member of the Charleston Southern University

---

15   Carrie Kreiswirth, "New E:60 Exclusive Delivers Powerful Message of Love and Forgiveness in Wake of Charleston Shootings," August 4, 2015, https://www.espnfrontrow.com/2015/08/new-e60-exclusive-delivers-powerful-message-of-love-and-forgiveness-in-wake-of-charleston-shootings/.

baseball team. Chris's mother was one of the victims of the tragic mass shooting at the Emanuel African Methodist Episcopal Church in Charleston, South Carolina. I have never been so moved by a television show about a message of love and forgiveness.

The following year I was in charge of a couples retreat for my local Young Presidents Organization (YPO) chapter. Thinking back on that ESPN episode, I thought, "What better way to spend a few days with those that we love than taking a deep dive on love and forgiveness?" So, I began planning the trip.

During that visit our group had the opportunity to meet with a man who also suffered loss from that tragedy. Anthony B. Thompson's wife, Myra, was one of the nine victims who lost their lives in the shooting. His path to forgiveness is a testament to the power of faith and love. Despite the unimaginable pain and grief he must have felt, Thompson chose to forgive the shooter. He stated that his faith in God and the teachings of the Bible inspired him to forgive and move forward.

But Thompson's forgiveness did not come easily. It was a long and painful journey that required him to confront his anger and pain head-on. However, through prayer and reflection, he found the strength to let go of his anger and hatred toward the shooter. Instead, he chose to focus on love and compassion, drawing strength from his faith in God. And it wasn't only Thompson: relatives of the Emanuel church victims' families stood up one by one in the courtroom at the shooter's bond hearing, offering forgiveness to the man accused of murdering their sons, mothers, and grandfathers in cold blood.

Many of the victims' families of the AME Church's path to forgiveness serves as an inspiration to all of us. It reminds us that even in the face of unspeakable tragedy and loss, we can find the strength to forgive and move forward. Thompson's story is a powerful reminder of the healing power of love and the importance of forgiveness in healing our wounds.

Forgiving is a reminder that we've all been forgiven. When Jesus Christ forgives, he says, "I don't see your sin anymore" (Colossians 3:13 MSG).

Forgiving is a skill that can be mastered. It is a learned skill that is a daily process without beginning or end. It is a process of letting go of hurts, helplessness, and anger while increasing confidence, hope, and happiness. It is a declaration that you will live your life on your terms, and no one person or situation is going to take that away from you. Once we are good at forgiving, it becomes such a simple practice. Maybe we made a mistake, but the lesson from that mistake actually makes us smarter for the future or wiser for the teacher.

Empathy

Empathy is the cornerstone to healthy high-functioning relationships. Empathy is more than an expression of sympathy; it's a deep understanding and a heartfelt connection to the feelings and emotions of others. People that feel empathy have a better outlook on life and a better connection to the world around them.

Without empathy we cannot move our hearts to a place of grace. Grace leads to freedom, and freedom allows us to love without the suffocating walls of judgment. Judgments lead to shame, and shame prevents empathy.

Grace is what makes us human—the better self that shines a light for others. Unfortunately, what is masqueraded by too many today is not true love. It is a love of convenience and ego. That is to say, it is the sentiment of "I will love you as long as you add value to my life and please me. When that ceases, so does my love for you."

In the city I live in, we have a big problem with people experiencing homelessness. There are many times I get frustrated by these people and times when I'm not living a heart-led life and get caught up in my selfish ways. But when I catch myself and live in an empathetic and heart-led manner, the feeling is amazing. This happened this past week as I was having lunch with a friend. As I was walking up to the restaurant, I noticed a man sitting on the sidewalk close by holding a sign that said, "Homeless vet. No job, no food." Rather than being frustrated and disingenuous, I decided to engage. The man was sitting with a woman, and I asked them if I could bring them some food, and if so, was there anything that they would like. When I brought the food out to them, I asked them if I could pray for anything for them. The man began to talk, and I just listened. He thanked me for the food and thanked me for just stopping. He went on to tell me that he had served in the Iraq war. When he returned he got a job but had a hard time keeping it. He said he still struggled with the war. As the economy tightened, his wife lost her job as well, along with their apartment and I'm sure their dignity. This man placed his life in harm's way for me and everyone in the USA. He thanked me repeatedly for the food for him and his wife and for stopping. I thanked him for his service. These two people didn't deserve my pity, only my respect.

Finding grace is the cornerstone to living and leaving a lasting legacy.

The Role of Love in Relationships

President Theodore Roosevelt is credited with the popular saying, "Nobody cares how much you know until they know how much you care." This is as true today as it was in 1912.

It means putting others before yourself. "You, my brothers, were called to be free. But do not use your freedom to indulge in the sinful nature; rather, serve one another in love. Love your neighbor as yourself" (Galatians 5:13–14 NIV).

Sometimes, it helps to think of it as "parking" your ego. Ego has no space in a relationship. Look at a mother and a new baby. There is no ego on either part—just pure adoration for each other.

American Franciscan priest and author Richard Rohr teaches that our primary operating system for the first half of our lives is the ego. And for the second half of our adult lives, it's our soul. I agree with this philosophy, but in our family our ego is grounded. My mother said, "I believe you have to have a little bit of an ego to be successful. You can't be wishy-washy. By this I mean you have to have opinions, but you have to be willing to admit when you're wrong. And you have to have the ability to say, 'I'm sorry. I made a mistake.' I think that's really important. Because you're never always right." (And then, of course she added, "Unless you're arguing with your husband, and then you're always right." Mom has always had a terrific sense of humor.)

Libraries are full of books that teach principles for healthy relationships, so I won't try to re-create any of them. All I can offer is that in my experience, healthy relationships start with trust and believing in one another.

I don't think I really appreciated what this really meant until I was a junior in high school. I was a quarterback on our high school football team, but I wasn't playing, because the starting quarterback was a senior and a far better quarterback than I ever was.

We had a really good team at that time, and we were playing an archrival toward the end of the season. It was a battle of a game; we were really struggling. We were down by six points late in the fourth quarter, and our quarterback led us to the three-yard line to set us up for a go-ahead score. Unfortunately, through the course of the play to get us there, he got hurt. I had to go in because I was the backup.

I was scared to death, because I hadn't played all season. I'd just been basically practicing up to then. The head coach came over to me, and he grabbed the grill of my face mask. He looked at me in the eye and said, "Listen. I believe in you, Young. You're good enough to do this. Go out and get us the touchdown."

And I went out and got us the touchdown. It's a moment that I will remember forever because it was the first time I remember anyone—outside of my family—ever saying anything like that. I believe in you. Now freaking go get it done. He trusted in me, and I lived up to that trust. This is the foundation of all good relationships.

> **WITHOUT LOVE, EVERYTHING YOU SAY AND DO IS INEFFECTIVE, EVERYTHING YOU BELIEVE IS INCOMPLETE, AND EVERYTHING YOU GIVE IS INSIGNIFICANT.**

I also find that healthy relationships are based around true friendship. A close friend shows love in any situation. Just like family, close friends can rebuke when necessary and do it in love. They keep us accountable.

One of the easiest ways to leave a legacy is to simply love. When we show up with our heart first, intentional and actionable insights will come. These insights will lead to legacies that will last for generations. It is only when we are heart first that we are able to receive and share love with others. Without love, everything you say and do is ineffective, everything you believe is incomplete, and everything you give is insignificant.

This may seem complicated, but being heart led is a matter of simple, day-to-day choices. It begins with having love toward every person in front of you. As the ancient Chinese philosopher Lao Tzu said, "Watch your thoughts, they become your words; watch your words, they become your actions; watch your actions, they become your habits; watch your habits, they become your character; watch your character, it becomes your destiny."

There is no greater value of the farmer's code than that of loving sacrificially and unconditionally.

seven

Grading

———

YOU CAN BECOME BLIND BY SEEING EACH DAY AS A
SIMILAR ONE. EACH DAY IS A DIFFERENT ONE, EACH
DAY BRINGS A MIRACLE OF ITS OWN. IT'S JUST A
MATTER OF PAYING ATTENTION TO THIS MIRACLE.

Paulo Coelho

The Farmer's Code

Once a crop is harvested, the farmer must then grade, sort, and pack the crop to be sold to the consumer. Grading the crop is the way we identify and separate the best of every crop from the less desirable produce so that we can make sure the best is what gets to the consumer. This takes careful observation and is one of the most important parts of the circle of the life for every farmer.

Observing the world around us and using consistent self-reflection is similar to this task in many ways. They both involve taking a critical and objective look at something (in this case, oneself or one's situation) to identify positive and negative aspects. When you look at yourself, you can identify strengths and weaknesses, make decisions that will best serve you and those around you, and take actions accordingly for improvement. In this sense, "grading" is yet another key to leaving a legacy.

See Others

A funny sitcom called *The Goldbergs* has an episode where teenage son Barry decides that he is so talented at karate that he has no choice but to show off his superior skills in the high school talent show. His mother, Beverly, sees his routine and is delighted, encouraging him vigorously. Problem is Barry has zero ability in the martial arts, and his routine looks more like the body spasms of a toddler tantrum than the finesse of a warrior. Beverly's "mom goggles" prevent her from seeing reality. All she sees is her "scrumptious," perfect boy. And of course hijinks ensue, and everything ends with a laugh.

In life outside of '80s sitcoms, this happens all the time. Have you ever attended an elementary school play? Or a middle school band concert? I have three kids, so I've attended many of them. If you ignore what's happening on the stage for a moment and watch the parents in the audience, mom and dad goggles are obvious. Enraptured parents and grandparents can't take their eyes off their supposed little prodigies for a second. I'm not saying this is a bad thing, by any means. But at some point most of us have to stop and look at the reality of what our darlings are actually capable of and what limitations they might have to acknowledge.

The opposite of this happens all the time as well. An old story tells how a young boy was so naughty to his kindergarten teacher that she documented his poor behavior thoroughly for the first grade teacher. Unsurprisingly, the boy continued to misbehave the next year and the next. This continued until the records got lost one year. Teachers had no idea what kind of students they would get, so they treated everyone equally. The boy suddenly went from "problem child" to "star pupil."

Of course this is just a fable, but it illustrates the point. We must see others for who they are and not what we want or imagine them to be.

See Ourselves

Human eyeballs generally contain a place where the optic cells in the retina cannot take in light, meaning that the field of vision is limited. This is called our scotoma, or blind spot. A simple exercise can help you discover where yours is. Just hold your thumb out in front of you at arm's length, close one eye, and focus on that thumb. Now hold the other thumb up at arm's length next to that thumb and slowly move it away, still focusing on the original thumb. At some point, the thumb in motion will get fuzzy and even disappear. This is the blind spot. You can do it with each eye, using the corresponding thumb. (Fun fact: squid eyes don't have them!)

What's interesting about blind spots is that our brains don't like to have an invisible spot in our field of vision, so they fill the space with information from the surrounding area. The brain basically makes a best guess as to what should be there, and we rarely if ever notice.

The same phenomenon happens with our psychological blind spots. Our brains don't like not knowing things, so they fill in the gaps with information as a best guess. Let's say, for example, that you can't see that the way you interact with other people in the mornings is negative and even caustic at times. Your blind spot prevents you from recognizing your own tone and words, along with the response that comes. Instead, you fill that gap with information that seems to make sense. You're just tired and need coffee before you start your day, just like everyone else. Perhaps this isn't reality, but it's what your brain chooses to tell you. And you believe it because you don't know any better.

Or let's say you constantly offer advice to others when it is not asked for. Your blind spot prevents you from seeing that your behavior borders on being rude, and instead you sincerely think you are being helpful. This habit can have a detrimental effect on your relationships, but unless someone points it out to you, you will blissfully continue to be "helpful" to everyone you meet.

WHAT ONE THING THAT, IF I CHANGED IT, WOULD MAKE THE BIGGEST DIFFERENCE IN MY LIFE?

In my family the younger generation was always taught to be humble and vulnerable about what we don't know. We aren't afraid to ask questions, because asking questions helps us see our blind spots. Taking your ego down is crucial if you want to improve in this way, but it makes you vulnerable. This is why trust is the foundation of every relationship. Ego and defensiveness are conjoined twins when one is looking for blind spots.

If it is too hard to ask others for their feedback at this time, I suggest starting by asking yourself this question: What one thing that, if I changed it, would make the biggest difference in my life?

Then get serious about the answer. Maybe it's one change in your habits? One change in your relationships? One change in your health? One change in your finances? If you changed just one thing, what difference would it make—really?

Reflect and Take Action

Once you have identified that one thing that you can do, do it! Focus your life on what's most important. Get rid of the distractions that challenge your one change. Enlist someone to hold you accountable, and hold onto the belief that one little change can change the world.

And once you have mastered that one change, reflect again, and repeat the process.

Self-reflection is the key to self-awareness. It allows us to look neutrally at our thoughts, feelings, emotions, and actions. It is the process of diving deep into our motivations and determining the "why" behind them.

There are great benefits to self-reflections, even though taking the time and effort to do it can be difficult. It allows you to gain great perspective. Because emotions can cloud our judgment and make us lose sight of what truly matters, things can seem bigger or worse than they really are. Self-reflection allows us all to take a step back and gain perspective on what really matters most and what needs to be ignored. It garners clarity.

Self-reflection also helps us respond to situations and other people more effectively. It is easy to react. I'll admit that I overreact or misreact at times, but I'm learning through self-reflection when my gut is telling me if my reactions are warranted or not. Personal reflection allows me to consider the consequences of my words and actions before and after the fact. It is a great way to garner and gain wisdom.

Without self-reflection we simply go through life without really thinking. We are in that survival mode, moving from one thing to the next without making time to evaluate whether things are actually going well.

My grandpa Ken taught my uncle Rick to be aware of his blind spots from a very early age. He said, "My dad was old school. He always thought you have to know everything about a task before you can tell anybody else how to do it. You better do it as good as you can first, and then you can teach other people how to do it. So, I was on backhoes and graders and tractors at twelve years old, learning what he knew I needed to know."

Legacy is developed from a life dedicated to self-reflection and purpose.

Observation Leads to Truth

A critical element of self-reflection is honesty. Those mom/dad goggles might be beneficial with a toddler or even a teenager, but they are detrimental in adult relationships with others and with yourself. Honesty can hurt, but you need to be true to yourself, and good things will happen, so do not be afraid to be honest.

I am a huge golf fan. Golf is considered by many to be a polite and respectful sport. It requires players to mind the rules with proper etiquette, while being honest, displaying good sportsmanship, and demonstrating respect for their fellow players. Incidentally, much like farmers, golfers also have a great respect for nature. I wonder if this is what drew me to the sport in the first place.

It is a sport I fell in love with when I was a kid. Growing up on the farm meant that my mom would only make one or two trips a week to the city for groceries and other errands. She seemed to find free childcare for me at one of the local golf courses. She would drop me off, and I would hit bucket after bucket of balls, play a few holes, and wear out my putter on the putting green while she did all the things in town she needed to do. I could lose time so easily that it always felt like she was only gone for minutes.

To this day I really enjoy losing track of time while on the golf course. I have also become a student of its history. Bobby Jones has long been considered one of the greatest golfers to ever play the game. While he wasn't a professional golfer, he is one of the most influential players because he was the first man in history to win what is called the "Grand Slam." To do this he won the British Open (the Open Championship), the US Open, and the US and British amateur championships all in one calendar year. In all he won thirteen of these championships in seven years. It should've been fourteen.

At the US Open in Boston, 1925, he hit his ball on the eleventh hole. After doing so he insisted that he had moved the ball slightly by accidentally clipping the grass. He told the officials that he had violated rule eighteen (moving the ball), but they didn't agree. He stayed firm, and they finally had to accept and gave him a one-stroke penalty. He lost the match by the same margin, one stroke. A sportswriter praised him for his honesty, to which he replied, "You might as well praise me for not robbing banks."

While Bobby Jones is considered one of the greatest to ever play the game, it is his honesty and integrity that make his legacy carry on today.

Observation Leads to Action

My dad had a deep respect for Grandpa Ken, even if they didn't always see eye to eye. He knew that Ken would say things as they were. He wasn't one to beat around the bush much. And this quality led others to trust in him all the more.

When discussing the irrigation and water issues of the state of California one night, my dad said, "Kenny was so far on top of the water insecurity that's happening here today. He could see it happening back when we were kids. He was a farmer, and he loved farming. He knew what it took, and he could just look around and see what was going on. He understood it. If things ever had anything to do with agriculture, Kenny could see what was coming."

Because Grandpa was always honest, he was open to hearing the truth from others, which led to making changes for the better. The same can be said for the amazing women who started the nonprofit organization where my wife works. Bakersfield Angels recognized a huge need in our community where we have high teen pregnancy, low graduation rates, and a large population of people experiencing homelessness. They took action by creating programs to wrap radical relational support around the foster care community.

This is but one example of where spirituality and character collide. This union leads to action in the world when our beliefs and values inspire us. The way in which we use our beliefs and values to shape our actions (and the actions of those around us) can have a strong impact on our own lives and the lives of others. This is the place where, if you have become self-developed enough, you can leave lasting fingerprints on all of your relationships, in your family, your organization, and your community. This is how legacies are built and is the cornerstone to living the farmer's code.

eight

Irrigating

NO MATTER WHAT PEOPLE TELL YOU,
WORDS AND IDEAS CAN CHANGE THE WORLD.

Robin Williams

The Farmer's Code

A farmer must provide quality water to their crops to ensure they receive the necessary nourishment to grow. In the state of California where I live, water is precious, so we plan and use only what is needed to keep the crop thriving. Plants die from overwatering just as much as underwatering, so there is a delicate balance that we have to keep in achieving the healthiest crop.

In a way, words are like water. Just as irrigating allows water to be directed to a specific area of intended growth, words can be directed to reinforce a specific message. Furthermore, irrigation can give life to crops that will feed and clothe the world, just as using words can add life and bring joy and clarity to a conversation or idea. To take the metaphor even further, irrigating large fields can be tedious and require consistent effort. Similarly, using the right words can be difficult and require thought and precision. Finally, just as improper and inefficient irrigation can lead to wasted water and resources, improper use of words can lead to misunderstandings and alienation.

Wise words, integrity, and truth require planning and attention while providing the necessary nourishment for effective and authentic self-expression. Words matter in leaving a lasting legacy.

Speaking Truth

My cousin Jane nailed it when she said, "We're a very truthful family. We are very comfortable with each other, telling it how it is. My aunt can tell me to go fly a kite, for example, and I can tell her to do the same. But it doesn't damage our relationship. I take that for granted sometimes."

This kind of honesty is unusual in large, multigenerational families, but I believe it is key to why we are still happily in business together. We don't pull any punches when it comes to speaking truth to each other, and we learned that from our grandfather. But we lead with love.

When I brought my wife home to meet my family for the first time, I was a little nervous about how she would handle the brutal honesty of Grandpa Ken. He was never one to mince words, so you never really knew what he would say. We walked into their living room, and I introduced Jennifer to him and GG.

He literally stepped back, slowly looked her up and down, then stepped back toward her. He reached out and turned her face to the side, and said, "Well, Michael, she's got the nose to be part of the family."

Jennifer burst out laughing and said, "Good thing I don't have a complex about my nose!"

Years later she can look back at this with delight.

> *Thankfully, I had a very direct father, so that didn't bother me. I had a really thick skin growing up, because I grew up in a house where there was a lot of teasing. So, it was funny to me when Ken was very direct and off the cuff. He would say things that might be really offensive to somebody else. It was a good thing I'm strong enough to take that.*
>
> *I was immediately drawn to how friendly and engaging the family was when I first met them. It impressed me how everybody asked questions. They were curious. They wanted to know about me. I loved that. His parents asked lots and lots of questions when he first brought me home.*
>
> *They had so many friends. I loved that they had community around them. The family is a force, for sure.*

We use honesty with humor to get our point across. Not the sarcastic, cutting humor that degrades everyone, but more the good-natured teasing that gently (or not-so-gently) puts people in their places when things start to get off kilter.

The ag world is full of people who know how to use good humor with truth, and we have used that trait in our family extensively. We focus on the honest truth, and if there is a touch of humor, all the better.

One of my favorite family stories is about Uncle Rick and Aunt Mary. They had the opportunity a number of years ago to visit Israel and walk the footsteps of Jesus in the Holy Land with the bishop of their church. It was a once-in-a-lifetime experience to see and feel the Bible come to life.

While in the city of Jerusalem, they had the opportunity to visit the Western Wall, also called the Wailing Wall. The wall is one of the holiest places in the Jewish religion and is believed to be the last remaining wall of the ancient temple built by King Herod more than two thousand years ago. It is a sacred place of pilgrimage and prayer.

Men and women worship separately at the wall. As my aunt and uncle approached their part of the wall, they both had a sense of peace that they had never felt. As Rick laid hands on the wall, he began to pray. As he put it, "I've never prayed so hard in my life; I really felt connected to God."

With his eyes closed and both hands firmly on the wall, he was lost in his euphoric prayer when he felt something warm hit his head and shoulder, breaking his solitude. He opened his eyes to realize a pigeon had just pooped on his head. He turned to the rabbi standing next to him and asked what it meant. The rabbi responded in all seriousness, "It's a sign from God. He thinks you are full of shit."

What better reminder not to take ourselves too seriously!

Words Can Lift

One of my favorite movies is *Dead Poets Society*, which came out in 1989. This film presents a great example of speaking truth, honesty, and using kind words. The main character, John Keating, encourages his students to look beyond the limits of their conservative boarding school and into a bright, unknown future. He urges them to "seize the day," to express themselves honestly, and to speak from the heart.

Throughout the movie Keating underscores the importance of being truthful and honest, while also being respectful and kind with their words. He encourages his students to write poetry and speak their truth as a way to better understand themselves and the world. In this way he demonstrates the power of truth, honesty, and kindness in connecting people to a higher sense of living.

Using words to uplift can be one of the most powerful, life-changing actions that we take. When my father was in Fort Lewis, Washington, for nine weeks before going to fight in Vietnam, he met a young woman who was a friend of a friend, and they dated a little bit before he deployed.

He said, "She's the one who got me through Vietnam because she wrote me at least one letter a day. And they were beautiful letters. I don't know what her major was in college, but she was just a prolific writer."

I am so thankful that my dad had someone like her in his life to bring him the words he needed to get him through that war. We all have the opportunity to do this for others. Maybe it's not writing letters like she did, but it can be over email, text, social media, or just talking. We all have the ability to lift and pour into others with our words.

Words Can Also Destroy

The opposite is true as well. You know the old saying, "Sticks and stones may break my bones …" The ending really should be "… words hurt worst of all." Words can create wounds that never heal. Wars can be started with words. People have been driven to unimaginable actions because of the words of others. My dad always says, "It's not the first angry word that starts an argument. It's the second one."

The same is true when it comes to self-talk. Sometimes we are our own worst enemy. "I can't do this," or "It's not worth the effort," or "Everyone else is better than I am."

Why do we do this? Well, biologically, it makes sense. After all, the human brain's main purpose is to keep us alive, so it focuses a lot of energy on staying safe and avoiding danger. That means we tend to worry too much about what could go wrong.

IT'S NOT THE FIRST ANGRY WORD THAT STARTS AN ARGUMENT. IT'S THE SECOND ONE.

As Darren Hardy, author of *The Compound Effect*, said, "Your brain is not designed to make you happy. Your brain has only one agenda in mind: survival. It is always watching for signs of 'lack and attack.' Your brain is programmed to seek out the negative—dwindling resources, destructive weather, whatever's out to hurt you … Your mind will stew on that all night long."[16]

I encourage you to be on the lookout for destructive words like "never" and "can't" and "not enough." When these and other negative thoughts appear, they take a toll on us.

Oscar-winning actress Jane Fonda gave a thought-provoking TEDx talk titled "Life's Third Act" where she said, "[If] you have, over time, reacted negatively to past events and people, neural pathways are laid down by chemical and electrical signals that are sent through the brain. And over time, these neural pathways become hardwired. They become the norm—even if it's bad for us—because it causes us stress and anxiety. If, however, we can go back and alter our rela-

---

16   Darren Hardy, *The Compound Effect* (Bhopal, India: Manjul Publishing, 2021).

tionship, re-vision our relationship to past people and events, neural pathways can change. And if we can maintain the more positive feelings about the past, that becomes the new norm. It's like resetting a thermostat."[17]

We can literally tell ourselves a new story, and that story can become our reality. We can speak and make things true.

I don't want to give negativity any more space than I have to in this book, but there is one more principle that I have to mention in the context of a family legacy. There is no gossip in a healthy family. Gossip murders people with words. Don't commit murder.

Wise Words

We all know movies where the mother, the father, the teacher, or the friend knows exactly what to say when the main character needs it most. But life isn't like the movies. When people we love are suffering, sometimes our minds go blank. We can't think of anything beyond vanilla platitudes to offer. "It's going to be OK" can be one of the least helpful phrases in the English language. But we use it all the time.

And honestly that's OK. What's most important is that they know we love them. The same is true when we have to tell hard truths. We need to communicate that we love them, despite their faults, and lift them up. We give the benefit of the doubt, and we offer grace. Truth without grace is mean. Grace without truth is meaningless.

> **TRUTH WITHOUT GRACE IS MEAN. GRACE WITHOUT TRUTH IS MEANINGLESS.**

---

17   Jane Fonda, "Life's Third Act," TED, accessed June 6, 2023, https://www.ted.com/talks/jane_fonda_life_s_third_act?language=en.

It can be tough to find balance between showing someone grace while making sure they know the truth. This doesn't mean there is no room for anger when delivering the truth. But it does mean that even if there is anger in the way you talk to someone, grace is inextricable from the truth.

We also have to be able to accept truth from others. Relationships are built on humility. When we realize we are wrong, we can extend grace to those that we have wronged and to ourselves.

Words have an immense power to shape our lives, deepen our understanding, and create meaningful communication between individuals in all facets of life. Although most of us understand this, it is often easy to forget the potential of language and writing. To be conscious of the full potential of our words, it is necessary to reflect expressly on their importance.

Words are crucial for communication. They are vital for meaningful exchange and discussion, as they help us satisfy questions, build relationships, and find understanding. As we become aware of their importance, we understand how it is vital for us to mindfully choose them. If a message is miscommunicated, or misunderstood, it is important to take responsibility for the words we have chosen to explain the situation. Mindful selection of the words we use helps create a successful dialogue and builds trust with the people we are interacting with.

Words are how we form and express our unique identities. We constantly use them to tell our stories and express our feelings, preferences, beliefs, and values. To be conscious of our own words is to be conscious of both our inner being and the message we are trying to convey. And, as we become conscious of the words we choose, we become less likely to make careless mistakes or hurtful comments.

It is also through words that we share history and shape our future. We use words to document the past, explain current trends and science, and develop our countries' and societies' values. We use them to communicate our deepest emotions and communicate our views on the world. Without the power of words, our cities, states, and countries would not be able to survive—without them, our societies would be silent, stuck in the same history without hope for a better future.

Truth is a part of communication like hydrogen is a part of water. Take it out, and you have something else. Something that does not nourish. Our communication should be nourishing in the choice of words that we use, both in quality and in quantity. Some in the younger generation enjoy teasing men of my generation about "mansplaining," the tendency for men of a certain age to go on and on and on about whatever it is they are saying, often when the audience already knows a great deal on the subject at hand. Sometimes even more than the speaker himself.

Abraham Lincoln once said, "It is better to remain silent and be thought a fool than to speak out and remove all doubt."

Words matter when leaving a legacy, because they provide insight, incite emotion, and capture the spirit of an individual. They help to tell the story of a legacy, revealing values, personality, and intentions, preserving them for future generations. Words give us the opportunity to express who we are and what we stand for, making a lasting impression of ourselves after we are gone. Words are key to developing a strong version of your own farmer's code.

LD A POSITIVE, PERMANENT *legacy*

OUGH DELIBERATE, *daily choices.*

PART 3

Impact the World (Them Now)

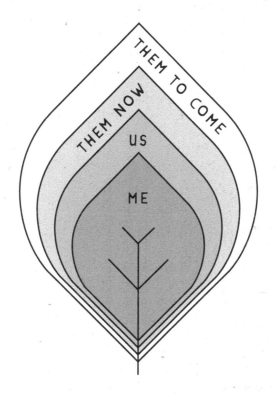

TO MANY PEOPLE SPEND THEIR LIVES BEING DUTIFUL
DESCENDANTS INSTEAD OF GOOD ANCESTORS.

Adam Grant

nine

Nourishing

WHEN THE PAST CALLS, LET IT GO TO VOICEMAIL.
IT HAS NOTHING NEW TO SAY.

Anne Lamott

The Farmer's Code

A farmer uses various techniques to restore and rejuvenate the land in order to preserve it for future generations. Farmers care for the soil by having a long-term perspective. This is what is called "generational thinking."

In the very real sense, dreaming, learning, and seeking wisdom are needed for legacy building. These are the elements that nourish the soil of our lives. When you identify your sense of purpose, you are acknowledging what you have to work with. When you dream and learn, you are thinking of the future.

Dreaming

Dreaming is the foundation of a legacy. It offers us the opportunity to think of the amazing things that can be achieved and gives us a reason to set our sights high. It inspires us to the possibility of what lies ahead in our lives if we are willing to reach. By dreaming, we can create our own aspirations and inspire others to dream too. We can also provide guidance and inspiration for others, leaving a powerful legacy by inspiring future generations to dream big too. Even Albert Einstein said, "Imagination is more important than knowledge."

Our family is 100 percent committed to letting everyone shine in their own way. My mother, Patti Young, said, "You must let each person shine on their own. You've got to let every person be the person that they are going to be to maximize their potential."

My uncle Rick has always been the real dreamer of the family, which has been a tremendous blessing to all of us. It was a trait he was probably born with, but it could have very easily been squashed. Having a family legacy means being willing to play supporting roles to the dreams of others as needed, just like my grandma and father did for Rick. When I was interviewing him for this book, he had some interesting insights about being the designated dreamer of the family and how tenuous that position was.

> *My mom always taught me that I could do anything I wanted to do, and I believed her because she was my mom. I've always said if I was on my own with my dad, I probably would not have gotten much done until he died.*
>
> *But if it wasn't for my brother-in-law and partner Richard, I probably would've got squashed. It was easier to dream because I had him behind me, worrying about working with the banks,*

worrying about the money, worrying about how to releverage, or do this or that. Even if my ideas failed, I always kept dreaming anyway. My relationship with Richard was the reason I started making the real dreams and risks to gain. I always felt that without Richard, I would've been one of two things: extremely wealthy or really broke. And it probably would've been the latter.

We go through cyclical times in agriculture. One minute everything is good. And the next it's terrible. Richard was taking all the beating in terms of having to deal with the emotional side of things. I know he was losing sleep to allow me to just keep dreaming.

Sometimes, I would wake up in the middle of the night with ideas. One time we started a tomato paste plant back in the late nineties and early two thousands. We were going to get out of the cotton industry and get more into the permanent crop industry, but because the permanent crops take so much money up front, you can't just dive into it. You'd never really make money until the seventh year, as a rule of thumb. Some crops, like pistachios, are ten to twelve years before you ever catch up to what your investment is. So it is a gradual thing.

A quicker way to change your farming operation and still be profitable is just to change to row crops. My friend, Jeff Fabbri knew the engineers who could build and run the plant. I knew all the growers. We realized we could put the money together and finance this thing.

The dreaming all of a sudden turned into reality. To build the tomato paste plant, we had all of our equipment coming from Italy, being shipped overseas into Long Beach. We had to haul all of this large equipment north to Buttonwillow. Mind you, that is a 150-mile drive on major freeways through Los Angeles. We were having to remove telephone lines and major power lines while parading these big, huge tanks into our little town of Buttonwillow, California.

As soon as you get the plant in place, you have to have the first crop ready to be harvested and processed. You can't wait one or two years to begin processing if you want to make a profit. So, we had $50 million worth of tomatoes sitting out there ready when the machines were being set up. If anything went wrong or there was a delay in the construction of the plant, we would have lost all those tomatoes. Those were some very tense days. We didn't know if we were going to pull this thing off or not.

One morning I looked out my living room window and could see the steam rising from the plant. We were up and running! In the coming days, I watched out my window every day. If a little steam was coming out of the top of it, then I knew the plant was running, but if there was a lot of steam pouring out, there was a problem, and we were shutting down. I started waking up in the middle of the night, running down there to make sure everything was OK. I lost a lot of sleep that first year.

It ran for a while, and then we got out just in time for the worst timing of the tomato paste market. There was a huge flood of carryover tomato paste worldwide. All of the investors in the tomato plant got their original equity back, but nobody made any money. We were only in about a thirty-five-dollars-a-ton market for our paste. Of course, today, it's one of the hottest things. It's $325 a ton. That's kind of what happens with a dream sometimes.

> *You might win or you might lose, but I figure it's always better to try.*

Rick has carried our family through some hard times, because he was willing to risk and follow his dreams, and he isn't the only one. We have all been given opportunities to share our vision for what the future might hold, and I am pleased to say that nobody is shut down. Sure, things might fail. But the damage that would come from closing those doors of creativity would last much longer than any mistake ever would.

Learning

Learning is another key element in leaving a legacy. It is what we need to do before we can develop our own dreams and ideas. It is also required to successfully navigate the world and life. We cannot possibly pass knowledge and understanding to the next generations if we don't take time to acquire it first. This doesn't always mean textbook kind of information. It can include our favorite quotes, stories, and advice that offer guidance on how to approach certain situations. Everything you know and everything you believe can be part of an inspiring legacy. What you learn in this book, for example, is a portion of your legacy journey.

I won't risk being tedious in listing all the ways that we can learn, other than to mention that we often overlook one source of knowledge that is always with us, and that is our own minds. Mindfulness research is proving all the time that we all have untapped insight built into our brains that can be accessed with the right mindset. It means being present in every moment and taking time out of our busy lives to savor in the quiet.

Practicing presence and living in the now are important parts of the farmer's code. Of course farmers learn from the past and worry about the future, but in reality they can only live in the now. They only know where their crop is right now, in this specific moment. What is the health of the plant today? That's all I can control. We watch over our crops in the here and now.

This is similar to self-awareness. Being in tune with the body keeps you in the here and now. For me I like to scan my body, head to toe, on a regular basis. How am I feeling? Do I recognize what feels good? What is tight? What hurts? Where are my thoughts?

I find when I ground myself in the here and now, gratitude always surfaces with an extreme sense of belonging. The gift of presence is the gift of peace. Belonging to God, belonging to one another, belonging to mother earth. This can't happen when we are mentally living someplace or somewhere else.

There is a great book called *Buddha's Brain* by Rick Hanson. In it Hanson says that Buddhists emphasize the importance of cultivating gratitude and compassion in living in the moment: "Gratitude can make life come alive. Compassion can help us stay present with challenging situations without getting lost in fear."[18]

As a Christian I find that by being present and having an intentional practice of expressing and embracing gratitude and compassion, I enrich my relationship with God. But I believe this can be the case with believers of any religion or faith system.

Author A. J. Jacobs wrote a book called *The Year of Living Biblically: One Man's Humble Quest to Follow the Bible as Literally as Possible*. In it he documents his experiences living according to biblical teachings as strictly as possible. After 365 days of singing hymns, praying, making sacrifices, letting his beard grow untrimmed, and

---

18   Rick Hanson, *Buddha's Brain* (Oakland, CA: New Harbinger Publishers, 2009).

even stoning adulterers and Sabbath breakers (hint: the Bible never says how big the stones have to be), he concluded the book with a reflection on what he would take away from the experience. He shared that as an ethnic Jew born to a very secular family, he was still unsure about his particular belief in God, or any specific religion for that matter. But the one thing he did know for certain was that thanking God in all things and at all times was a practice he intended to keep up. There are many scriptures that give us this guidance, including 1 Thessalonians 5:16–18 ESV that says, "Rejoice always, pray without ceasing, give thanks in all circumstances …"

Keeping the commandment of constant gratitude changed A. J. for the better, and it can do the same for us. Imagine the joy that could come into our lives if we were always thanking him, no matter how insignificant the blessing. Our lights come on when we flip a switch. Thank you, God. We have clean water from the tap. Thank you, God. I slept safely in my own bed all night. Thank you, God. This kind of gratitude requires a constant awareness of every moment, taking nothing for granted.

Seeking Wisdom

King Solomon is known as the wisest man in history. His greatest desire was to be wise, so he sought wisdom both through study and prayer until God came to him and offered to grant him any wish. When he asked for wisdom, God was pleased and granted him a wise and discerning heart. In addition to seeking guidance from God, Solomon studied philosophy and was an avid reader, expanding his knowledge of the world. He consulted with wise mentors and elders to help him understand the complexities of ruling a kingdom. All these efforts combined helped to make him one of the wisest and most learned of all kings. Even the Queen of Sheba sought him out to mentor her.

Unfortunately, that wisdom was also his downfall. He forgot to nurture his spiritual needs by keeping the commandments of God. Power and politics became his god. He may have been the smartest, richest, most powerful man on earth at the time, but according to the book of Kings, he died in disfavor with God. His magnificent temple was looted and destroyed, his sons were executed, and his people were taken into slavery. Not a single piece of archaeological evidence remains of what he spent his entire life building.

When you are grounded in the present, you can offer the gift of presence with those around you, and, more often than not, when you offer presence to others, they offer it right back to you. When this happens, you will have the ability to offer, seek, and hear wisdom.

WE MUST STOP REHASHING THE PAST OR FRETTING ABOUT THE FUTURE BEFORE WE CAN BE PRESENT.

Wisdom can only be sought by living in the present, being in the moment. We must stop rehashing the past or fretting about the future before we can be present. Don't mistake my message here though. Pondering the past is an important part of understanding who we are; just don't live there. The past is a great place to learn from but a terrible place to live. Growth doesn't happen by being stuck in the past.

Growing up, if we had a choice to go to Grandma or Google to get a question answered, I think we would all go to Grandma. That's what makes us different. We want to learn and tap the wisdom of our elders. I like to think of wisdom as metabolized experience, which leads to distilled compassion. That metabolized experience leads to understanding yourself and the world more, which allows us to have some level of compassion, because wisdom without compassion is just doing something for yourself. And being selfish doesn't leave a legacy.

Relators often say, "Location, location, location." That is a spiritual mantra as much as it is a real estate mantra. When we live in the past or future, we are not really here. When we aren't really here, we can't access wisdom.

Wisdom, simply put, is skilled and applied knowledge that is gained through personal experiences and from those of other people. It reminds me of the old saying, "Knowledge is knowing that a tomato is a fruit; wisdom is knowing not to put it in fruit salad." It is a valuable asset that can be used to help guide others as well as us. By taking the time to seek out wisdom, we can learn valuable lessons that can help us to understand the world and its challenges. This wisdom can then be shared with others, providing an invaluable part of a legacy.

German spiritual teacher Eckhart Tolle does a great job articulating basic Christian truths that we have forgotten. If you really look through the Bible, you can see that Jesus didn't answer many of the questions he had thrown at him. He actually answered just a few. We can see that he provided space for the questioner to use their own resources to find answers rather than depend on him for guidance. They had the power to find that wisdom if they had enough space.

Jesus always came back to one essential reminder. "Where are you right now?" The house of God is in the present. We can't access him in the past, and we can't access him in the future. The only place to find God is in the here and now. This "now" moment is the moment to be with God. Jesus said the kingdom of God is in the here and the now. It's not one day in the future. He taught us to pray, "Thy kingdom come, Thy will be done in earth [now], as it is in heaven" (Matthew 6:10 KJV).

In Andy Stanley's book *Ask It*, he challenges us to ask a simple question every day about the choices we face. This question makes it easy to determine the answer to all other questions we might encounter, and it allows us to make decisions with confidence. It is the simplest question in the world: "Is it wise?"

Super easy and basic. More importantly it is the easiest path to wisdom.

Asking, "Is it wise?" is both simple and hard in every decision in life. Why is it hard? Because it is hard to be honest with ourselves. When we are honest with ourselves, we reveal our true intent, and let's be honest: self-deception can give us pretty much anything we want. We can convince ourselves bad relationship choices look like we can "save" another person. We can make bad investments sound like investment opportunities. We can rationalize doing the wrong thing for what we think to be the right reason.

You need wisdom to build relationships. You need wisdom to be the light in your workplace. You need wisdom to lead your family. You need wisdom to leave a legacy. Without it, what are you passing on?

In the Bible, James says, "If any of you lacks wisdom, you should ask God, who gives generously to all without finding fault, and it will be given to you" (James 1:5 NIV).

Wisdom is one of our family strengths. The younger generations are allowed to play to their strengths while guided by the wisdom of the older generations. To leave a lasting legacy, you must first allow wisdom into your life, then be willing to share that wisdom as you move on into later years.

Wisdom produces three things in my experience: character, competence, and connection. Character gives us the ability to be wise and skillful in ethics and morals. Competence guides our actions as we go about our day-to-day tasks. Connection allows us to interact with each other and to be skillful in personal and professional relationships.

Connection is the very foundation of leaving a legacy. Everyone matters, so instead of just leaving a mark on them, you have the opportunity leave a great mark on them. This is what legacies are made of. Relationships are the foundation to the farmer's code.

Fertilizing

The Farmer's Code

Fertilizers have been used by farmers to supplement the nutrients in the soil for centuries. There is evidence that they have been used as far back as the stone ages. Today, fertilizers include amendments of all kinds, from leaves and manure to complex synthetics. Proper fertilization requires a careful assessment of the health and nutrient level of each plant for optimal growth. Fertilizing a crop involves taking a humble and open approach to learning and improving, knowing that you aren't going to get it right every time.

Just as a plant needs the proper balance and nutrition to grow, human beings need the same for a successful "harvest." Leaving a legacy requires the amendments of special nutrients to the "code" of your life, particularly the right blend of humility mixed with the ability to listen to others. Both require careful assessment and are essential for personal growth and the development of lasting relationships.

Listening

Alfred Brendel started learning piano lessons when he was six years old in Croatia. His family moved to Austria, where he continued with his piano lessons until he was sent to dig trenches in Yugoslavia when he was fourteen during World War II. He had a few more lessons after the war was over, but his spotty training ended. For most people that would be the end of the musical journey, but for Brendel it was just the beginning.

He continued his piano studies on his own and gave his first public recital at seventeen. On the official website of Alfred Brendel, he is quoted as saying, "A teacher can be too influential. Being self-taught, I learned to distrust anything I hadn't figured out myself." He found that listening to the music of other pianists, conductors, and singers was far more valuable than anything he could learn from a teacher. He also made a practice of listening to himself. He would record himself playing each piece of music and then spend hours listening to himself and studying what he heard.

He is one of the most celebrated pianists of our time and holds the distinction of being the first pianist to record the entire works of Beethoven and one of only a few who have ever recorded all of the Mozart concertos. Among the laundry list of accolades in his life, he has been knighted by Queen Elizabeth; awarded honorary doctorates from Oxford, Yale, Cambridge, Juilliard, and many other schools; and given five lifetime achievement awards. All because he listened. He is quoted as saying, "The word 'listen' contains the word 'silent.'"

This point is so often lost. When we participate in conversations, it is so easy to fall into the habit of half listening. Just waiting for our turn to talk. As Simon Sinek put it, "There is a difference between listening and waiting for your turn to speak."

THE WORD "LISTEN" CONTAINS THE WORD "SILENT."

There are books full of advice on how to engage in active listening, all of which emphasize the importance of paying attention first and foremost. We validate those we are with when we really listen, letting them know by our nonverbal cues that what they are saying matters to us.

Our ability to multitask is our undoing when it comes to really listening. How often do you look at your phone when your spouse or child or friend or colleague is speaking to you? Just a moment, you think. Just to glance at that notification you just got. The speaker fades into the background as you get absorbed in the Insta post or the email, and you absentmindedly nod and mumble agreements with whatever is being said. They walk away, and you realize you have no idea what they said in the end. Hopefully it wasn't important.

What matters less is the subject that they were talking about and the way you just made them feel. Your inability to listen to all of what they wanted to share with you means you placed them below your phone in rankings of importance. Don't believe me? Studies show that people wildly overestimate their ability to listen effectively.

In the book *The Plateau Effect: Getting from Stuck to Success*, authors Bob Sullivan and Hugh Thompson cite a study that asked volunteers to sit through a ten-minute presentation. Then they were asked to describe what they had just listened to. Half of the participants failed. They were asked again after two days, and "fully 75 percent of listeners" couldn't repeat what they had heard. The reason they put forth is that our brains are capable of understanding about four hundred words a minute. Nobody can talk that fast, so when we listen, we have a significant part of our cognitive ability that is not being used. Rather than sitting idle, our brains find ways to stay occupied, from listening to the conversation at the table next to us to planning what we are going to do that night.

Children, as easily distracted as they seem, are actually far better listeners than adults. Sullivan and Thompson cite a study conducted by Ralph Nichols, a professor of rhetoric at the University of Minnesota.[19] He asked elementary, middle school, and high school teachers to stop partway through their lessons and ask students to describe what the teacher had just been saying. First and second graders were able to accurately recall what the teacher was saying 90 percent of the time. Junior high students were down to 44 percent, and high schoolers dropped to about 25 percent. The older we get, the less we listen.

But it doesn't have to be that way. Rule number one is to put the phone away. Study after study has proven that even if we aren't using it, the mere presence of a phone reduces our cognitive capacity. Put it out of sight.

Next, be mindful of your physical presence. Are you crossing your arms and legs? Are you turned half away, or are you presenting your whole, open self to the person you are talking to? When you open yourself up and really look at them, you will likely find they are more willing to share with you. Eye contact, nodding, agreeing,

---

19   Bob Sullivan and Hugh Thompson, "Now Hear This! Most People Stink at Listening [Excerpt]," May 3, 2013, https://www.scientificamerican.com/article/plateau-effect-digital-gadget-distraction-attention/.

and smiling can be powerful cues for the speaker that you are actually listening to them.

Then, close your mouth. The less we speak, the more we listen. It sounds obvious, but if you're thinking about what story you want to share as soon as you get a break in the conversation, you are not actively listening. Be OK with silence if the conversation falls into a lull, and allow the other person or people to reflect with you on what they just said. You will likely find that the next thing they share is more meaningful than what they previously said.

Finally, if you find it difficult to continue to pay attention, think to yourself, "I love this person. I want only the best for them." Highly renown international speaker Julian Treasure said that "it isn't possible to judge someone and wish them well at the same time."

There is a staple activity of the improvisational comedy world called "Yes, And." In this game actors stand in a circle and are given only one instruction. Every time someone says something, they have to eagerly respond, "Yes, and …"

For example, the first player might say, "I have a sweet dog."

The next player will respond, "Yes, and he is very big."

Then the game continues with each player adding on to the story.

"Yes, and he takes up the whole room."

"Yes, and he keeps chewing on the furniture."

"Yes, and he doesn't really have any fur."

"Yes, and he is crashing through the walls now."

"Yes, and I just realized that my dog is actually a dinosaur."

"Yes, and we are all running for our lives!"

Then the group will actively run away with delight.

You get the idea. The fun of the game is to listen carefully to the story and add a new detail that will take it in a fun direction, without judgment as to what the previous statement was.

In daily life it is so easy to default to no. So much easier than trying to listen and understand what someone else is asking from us. The idea of "yes, and" is a tool that can allow us to pause, listen, and create something new from what someone else is offering. This attitude of "yes, and" can be (and has been) applied to personal and business relationships. The skill of active listening is a powerful fertilizer that can improve the development of every relationship in your life, leaving a legacy of respect and love.

Humility

There is an anonymous story that has been circulating for nearly a century, but it merits retelling. A giant ship sat docked at port with a failed engine, losing money with every passing day. The owners of the ship brought on board one expert mechanic after another, but none of them could figure out what was wrong.

At the end of their list was an old-timer who had been fixing ships for decades. He shuffled on board with a large bag of tools, taking his time as he inspected the engine.

When he was done, the old man unzipped his worn bag and pulled out a single hammer. He reached down into the engine and tapped once. Instantly, the engine sprang back to life. He put his hammer away and tottered back to the docks.

The owners of the ship received a bill from him for $10,000.

The owners were shocked and refused to pay him, demanding a revised bill with an itemized explanation of his services.

The man returned the bill with a note that read:

Tapping with hammer: $2.00

Knowing where to tap: $9,998.00

The moral of the story is obvious. Effort is important, but knowing where to put that effort makes all the difference.

Don't let confidence be confused with arrogance. There is a clear distinction. A humble person does not lack confidence; they simply channel their confidence into relationships and productivity rather than displaying their ego. An arrogant person is only confident in themselves and their abilities, completely disregarding others. A confident person can comfortably share any space with others, secure in themselves and their abilities. Ryan Holiday writes in his book *Ego Is the Enemy*, "Impressing people is utterly different from being truly impressive."

Arrogance finds a way to fill a room, but humility knows how to coexist in harmony with ambition and confidence. One can be proud and assertive while being humble. The difference is the ego. Letting pride rule makes us insincere, while humility makes us real. As Confucius says, "Humility is the solid foundation of all virtues."

I ruptured my Achilles tendon on my fiftieth birthday during a game of pickleball. The recovery process caused me to rely on people more than I ever have. More importantly it really made me wake up to the importance of asking for help. Often one of the hardest things for us to say is, "I need help." It is so easy to get caught up in our own pride to the point that we would rather stay silent than ask for help. It has become human nature to say we're not hungry until the day that we starve. This is a habit we need to break. It is OK to ask for help. Have the courage to raise your hand if you need help. As you do so, the people around you will not only be able to help you, but will also have increased feelings of importance in your life. You never have to fight alone.

To be humble is to be willing to learn, receptive to correction, and open to a higher calling. Self-development is risky and scary at times, but we need to ask ourselves, "If I keep living the way I am living, who will I be at one hundred?" My grandmother is one hundred years old now, and she tells everyone that the only thing that really matters in life is the relationship you have with those you love. Everything else fades away. Humility means we are willing to adapt and change for those we love.

Humility is also knowing your strengths and your weaknesses without shame. It is being proud of "this is who I am, this is what I am good at, and this is what I am not good at." When you know what you are good at, you have found your superpower, but this will also be your blind spot if you are not self-aware.

Humility welcomes collaboration, and arrogance blocks it. What has made us successful as a family is that we understand each family member's strengths and weaknesses. We lift up the strengths and fill in for the weaknesses with our own superpowers. For me, my superpower is seeing the big picture. This also lends to my blind spot of skipping over details and cutting corners. Because of this I understand that I need people in my life that are good at details. Where I lack in detail, my dad is an expert. He dives deep into the research, but he also understands that he has a hard time seeing the forest through the trees. Where my cousin is amazing at listening to others and collaborating, he understands that he can be too accommodating and needs partners to help carry him through his blind spots. It takes self-awareness backed by humility to see and embrace both your superpowers and blind spots. My aunt Mary Wegis said, "We put our pants on one leg

> HUMILITY WELCOMES COLLABORATION, AND ARROGANCE BLOCKS IT.

at a time, the same way everybody else does. If you ever get hoity toity, you're not going to make it in this world."

Saint Augustine said, "It was pride that changed angels into devils; it is humility the makes men as angels." To leave a lasting legacy, every person should inspire, train, and go out of their way to set their relationships up for success. This will positively impact future generations. Without humility, this turns from a challenging to impossible task.

Legacy building means living a life centered on putting the needs of others before our own. It means making sure everyone else has what they need to meet their goals and grow as a human. This also means understanding our reality and our current situation, including our own strengths and weaknesses. To live the farmer's code, one must have developed listening skills and humility as key tools in one's toolbox.

LD A POSITIVE, PERMANENT *legacy*

OUGH DELIBERATE, *daily choices.*

PART 4

Living Your Legacy

(Them to Come)

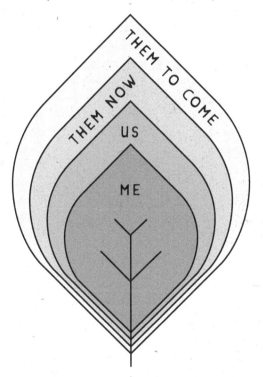

I KNOW THAT THE ONLY WAY TO LIVE MY LIFE IS
TO TRY TO DO WHAT IS RIGHT, TO TAKE THE LONG
VIEW, TO GIVE OF MY BEST IN ALL THAT THE DAY
BRINGS, AND TO PUT MY TRUST IN GOD.

—*Queen Elizabeth II*

eleven

Protecting

WHEN SOMETHING FEELS OFF, IT IS.

Abraham Hicks

The Farmer's Code

Have you ever seen a tomato hornworm? How about an Asian citrus psyllid? If you haven't, brace yourself before you look them up. They are some of the most creepy of the crawlies found in the California ag lands where we farm.

Pest infestations are one of the most persistent threats to farming. Bugs like grasshoppers, aphids, caterpillars, beetles, and mites can chew through leaves, stems, and roots, which can weaken or kill the plant. They carry and spread diseases and block a plant's photosynthetic tissues, reducing its ability to produce energy and grow. All of this can (and often does) impact the overall yield, and in worst cases it will destroy a crop. Think about the locust devastations that keep happening in Africa. A farmer must protect their crops from pests and disease in order for them to flourish.

Farmers are constantly monitoring and discerning good and bad by carefully observing their crops and assessing the condition, growth, and health of the plants. This can include but is not limited to testing soil, monitoring weather and weather patterns, as well as staying on top of pests and diseases. As we monitor we improve our ability to make informed decisions about our farms and the investments we make in them.

Legacy builders do the same. First, we have to get rid of the pests and flush any leftover toxins from our lives. Once we are rid of the infestation, we must be willing to look carefully at the exposures and vulnerabilities we might have to further risks. It's that old "set your house in order" philosophy—get things straight in your life, and then protect it so that you can maintain growth and share it with others.

When I say infestation, I am not necessarily referring to bugs—however, you may have factors in your life that are bugging you that you should address. What I mean is taking into account all of the threats you have discovered throughout this book that make you a less-than-ideal example to future generations. Compare that with the type of influence you leave when you are healthy, happy, fulfilled, and completely actualized. As you work to reach the highest stage you possibly can, you have to fortify yourself so you don't backslide. This is what I mean by protection.

Monitoring and protecting are similarly important in our personal lives in terms of self-development. We can watch, study, examine, and make choices around the investments we take with our own thoughts, actions, and behaviors. This is legacy work at its very foundation. This is the farmer's code.

Discernment

On July 21, 1952, a massive earthquake hit the San Joaquin Valley, where Bakersfield is located. My mom was five, and her brother—my uncle Rick—was three. This was just after World War II, so everyone was still living in the war mindset.

The quake sent the countryside into a deep darkness, periodically flashing with the eerie lights of substations catching fire. My grandmother said, "When we saw those transformer explosions, we just instinctively thought we were being bombed."

Thankfully, this was not the case, but you can see how mindset can warp our sense of reality when we try to discern without having all the facts.

Discerning good from bad takes practice. It is rare to learn any skill and master it from the very start. Malcolm Gladwell famously wrote in his book *Outliers* that it takes roughly ten thousand hours of practice and experience to become a true expert in anything. We must practice, practice, practice. Everything from tying your shoes to riding a bike to learning to speak another language to learning God's word. It takes time and practice to become competent.

The conscience, when properly trained, is a great tool in discernment. If your conscience calls into question the effectiveness or value of what you are doing, you should stop and consider your actions carefully. Once you have recognized through discernment that there are things that are not helping (or even hurting) your progress, it is up to you to eliminate those factors as best you can. Avoid the toxic things in your life, and seek the good.

Here are some practical ways I discern good from bad:

- Seek advice from multiple sources. If everyone is telling you the same thing, it is either a wise move to make or your network is full of yes men. To ensure it isn't the latter, make sure you have a diverse pool of resources.

- Consider your sources' self-interest. Make sure to keep top of mind what agenda or bias might be driving the advice of your sources.

- Listen to everyone. Other people will have insight, expertise, and experiences that you don't have. Extract as much value from everything as you can. There is no point in reinventing the wheel or making the same mistake they did. That is how wisdom is developed.

- Interrogate the *shoulds*. I have a group of close friends that meet monthly to discuss business and personal issues. They are my personal board of directors of sorts. Our rule is to never *should* on someone. When people give advice, they often "should" or "shouldn't" you. Know that those *shoulds* often reveal a lot about another person's values, desires, or rules. I like to replace the word *should* with *could*. It removes the judgment that one course of action is superior to another.

- Trust your gut. If it feels right, it probably is. The Holy Spirit won't lead you down the wrong path. Your gut and intuition rarely lie, and they can be a valuable compass as you walk through life.

Love also helps discern what is good. The way in which we love shows the difference between good and bad. The apostle Paul says, "Love must be sincere. Hate what is evil; cling to what is good" (Romans 12:9 NIV). When Paul says, "Love must be sincere," this type of love is not the same as an emotional "butterfly" feeling you get when you are around someone you are attracted to. This is a deeper, more genuine, more godly form of love.

My uncle Rick Wegis commented on something GG always taught us: "Don't be married to your land, your assets, or any of your things. As you get older, you're going to find that that has no value in life. The value of life is the relationship you have with your family and those closest to you. It is what you do to improve those relationships—that is where the real prosperity lies."

In short those who take your time and your energy are by default your priorities. Not taking into account the hours you have to be at work, consider how many hours you spend with the people you think are your priorities versus the hours you spend with others. Are you with your children as often as your friends on your off hours? Are you with your spouse as much as your buddies? Do you linger with your coworkers after work when you could be home with your family? This is part of the discernment process. What kind of effect is that having on you and your family? I know one of the reasons our family business has lasted four generations is that we honor our priorities.

I don't use the word "hate" much in my normal conversations, but I think it is worth noting the strength of this word here. It isn't just "ignore," "shut down," or "tolerate" that which is evil. Paul instructs us to reject it the way we would reject poison in our food. We are being encouraged to get rid of any evil influence in our life.

This is where boundaries come in.

Boundaries

The fruit of the spirit gives us a strong and uncompromising set of values that can strengthen our ability to "do the right thing." Are you someone who can be trusted to do what you say you will do and to live up to the principles you claim to believe in? Do you have enough character and grounding in your spirituality to turn away elements that are not beneficial for you or for those around you?

My dad said, "Rick and I have been partners for forty-five years. During that time we have made some bad decisions, but our good decisions have been better than our bad ones. Our cheapest education was college. The money you make and lose making decisions, learning how to do the business you are in, is where your real education is."

They both grew because they knew that the tension of differences was a benefit and not a detriment. Healthy boundaries grow from knowing yourself well enough to know what kind of people raise you up and what kind of people drag you down. If you are an optimistically effervescent kind of person, you might want to remember that fountains attract drains. In the business world, we often hear that 20 percent of the people cause 80 percent of the problems. Those 20 percent are the people who will drain you dry.

All relationships have effects on you, both positive and negative. Don't be afraid to learn from them all. Focus on self-improvement, and stay away from the noise. There are times when we want to move on from relationships that aren't working so that our energy can be used in the most effective ways possible. Give yourself permission to move away from people who don't bring any value to your life.

It is impractical to cut out every single negative person, of course. The best thing we can do is try to surround ourselves with people we can trust, who will build us up and not tear us down. And to be that person in return.

Discernment is a complex yet vital skill and a key component of the farmer's code. It requires patience and a willingness to consider multiple perspectives to make the best decisions. It's the same as nurturing a crop all the way through harvest.

Nurturing the ability to discern is essential to having a healthy lifestyle. By continuing to practice monitoring, observing, assessing, and taking the appropriate action, individuals can strengthen this quality over time. Through this practice we can become better communicators, better leaders, better listeners, and better advocates for ourselves and others.

In the end having an unwavering practice of discernment enhances our lives in all areas, making us better equipped to handle life's challenges. Discernment leads to positive impact, which leads to creating a brighter future and a lasting legacy.

This step is a difficult one for many people to make, especially for kind-hearted people pleasers. They tend to believe the best in everyone and give people the benefit of the doubt as a default. This can sometimes get people into trouble, because unfortunately there are energy vampires in the world.

Remember, all relationships have effects on you, both positive and negative. Never be afraid to analyze what these effects are and learn from them. There will come a time when you will want to move on from some relationships that may not benefit you anymore. I encourage you to figure out now the best ways to spend your energy. Give yourself permission to "flush the toxins" by distancing yourself from people who don't bring anything to your life. Think about how personal boundaries can align with your values to bring you a greater sense of peace in your relationships with less resentment and negativity.

When you do this, it is important to be forgiving and willing to drop judgment. When we judge and hold onto grudges, we are only hurting ourselves. Sitting high on the throne of judgment only draws a line between "them" and "us." This division is a cause of unneeded stress. As GG says, "If you hold a grudge, you are just making yourself miserable."

Unwillingness to forgive is like poison to our souls. My father explains the family philosophy that "everything affects you, even if you say it doesn't. It's just how you react to the effect that frames the story." He shared how he came to appreciate this from my uncle. "When someone wrongs Rick, he forgets and moves on. For me it isn't as easy. I can move on, but it is a strike against the wrongdoer. I'm more cautious about how I move through life, so while I can let go of hurts, it takes more time."

I really like Rudyard Kipling's poem about balance titled "If—." It is a great example of how to leave a legacy. In this poem he advises his son to move through life with composure and to always exercise self-control, integrity, and humility. An excerpt of the poem reads,

> *If you can keep your head when all about you*
> *Are losing theirs and blaming it on you,*
> *If you can trust yourself when all men doubt you,*
> *But make allowance for their doubting too;*
> *If you can wait and not be tired by waiting,*
> *Or being lied about, don't deal in lies,*
> *Or being hated, don't give way to hating,*
> *And yet don't look too good, nor talk too wise ...*
> *Yours is the Earth and everything that's in it*

Kipling concludes his poem with a promise the "Yours is the Earth and everything that's in it." What more beautiful goal can there be? Obviously, a single poem can't possibly outline all the qualities and behaviors that one should possess to be a strong, honorable, and successful individual, but it is certainly a start!

Negative Capability

John Keats is remembered for being an accomplished English poet, producing lines like, "A thing of beauty is a joy forever," and "The poetry of Earth is never dead." He is often overlooked as the wise coiner of the term "negative capability." This phrase is a way to express a person's ability to tolerate uncertainty and embrace ambiguity when dealing with life's complexities. He used it in praise of the greatest writers he knew as the key ingredient to creative genius; this included William Shakespeare.

In a letter to his brothers, he pondered what it took to be a person of greatness, a "man of achievement," as he put it. Here is an excerpt from the letter:

> *What quality went to form a Man of Achievement ... possessed so enormously—*
>
> *I mean Negative Capability, that is when a man has the capacity to accept paradoxes and contradictions without attempting to reconcile or explain them away ...*[20]

Granted, the language Keats used was lofty and, to some, a bit too complex for our modern preferences, but the sentiment he expresses is as relevant now as it was in 1817, when he wrote it. He is referring to the ability to be comfortable in the process of confusion. This skill seems to be growing more rare as the echo chambers scream ever louder today. But there are some who set a terrific example by being willing to let mysteries remain mysterious and for opposing views to sit with equal importance in their mind.

---

20   John Keats, "The 'Negative Capability' Letter," George Mason University, accessed June 6, 2023, https://its.gmu.edu/find-a-service/?customel_dataPageID_4609=7459.

This capability includes humility, patience, curiosity, and critical thinking all in one. It means taking time to work things out for oneself. Just because we listen to and learn from divergent viewpoints doesn't mean we must abandon what we know to be true. On the contrary, it often means we are more solidly on a personal path of discovery and that it is OK to let two opposing views play in our minds simultaneously. We don't allow our very natural desire for order to hijack the process of learning.

My father had a great deal of negative capability when he partnered with my grandfather and his brother-in-law, my uncle Rick. Together, they were OK with the tension of differences. More than OK, in fact. They found it to be a blessing. Dad said, "Rick and I have had one argument in forty-five years. The reason it worked is because of our flaws. Rick has flaws, and my flaws are opposite of his flaws; together, we almost make the perfect person! Well, not perfect, but close. His weaknesses are my strengths, and mine are his. It allowed us to pass that on to the next generation as well."

> JUST BECAUSE WE LISTEN TO AND LEARN FROM DIVERGENT VIEWPOINTS DOESN'T MEAN WE MUST ABANDON WHAT WE KNOW TO BE TRUE.

Give yourself the grace to be wrong and imperfect. In order to develop relationships with others, especially those who are emotionally immature, we first have to deal with our own stuff. That takes grace and empathy to forgive ourselves and others. Make the best decisions you have with what you know. If you are marching down a path and you think you need to change course, then do it. Just don't spend an inordinate amount of time trying to make the perfect decision or waiting for the perfect advice.

And it all starts with knowing what is and what is not helpful to you, personally. Discernment is crucial to living the farmer's code.

Cultivating

twelve

TO IMPROVE IS TO CHANGE, SO TO BE
PERFECT IS TO HAVE CHANGED OFTEN.

Sir Winston Churchill

The Farmer's Code

To deliver a great harvest, the farmer is always cultivating the land. Cultivation is another way to say developing or working on the land. It includes anything required for the land to be prepared for planting and raising crops. Cultivation requires patience and long-term thinking via a proper plan and strategy.

When cultivating a legacy, one of the skills needed is learning to do what you say you are going to do, or as some people say, "walking the walk." The act of cultivation in farming and "walking the walk" in life both involve taking consistent and persistent actions to achieve a desired outcome. It means acting, not waiting to be acted upon. Cultivation is everything needed to prepare for a legacy.

Prepare Now

Why am I talking about preparation a dozen chapters in? Regardless of whether you are at the beginning of your adult life or at the end, your ability to leave a legacy begins today. Right now. It starts with looking back over everything that you have read in this book so far and actually using it. This means that you need to stop and reflect on what you have learned and take action now. Get back to work.

You may have heard an old story about the two woodcutters who had a competition to see who could chop the most wood in one day. They began in the morning, both chopping trees down as fast as they could in different locations in the forest. They couldn't see one another, but they could hear each other's axe blows as they struck.

An hour in, one of them stopped chopping for fifteen minutes. The other woodcutter got excited about this silence, assuming his opponent was already taking a break. He quickened his pace, proud of his own strength. The other man's chopping resumed at a steady rate, but then again, there was silence. The other woodcutter felt even more pleased as he kept his fast pace.

This pattern continued until the end of the day. As the sun set, the man who had not stopped finally stood back to proudly survey his pile of wood, knowing he had won the competition. He walked over to see the size of the other man's pile, only to find that it was twice the size.

He angrily accused his opponent of cheating. "I heard you stop chopping for at least fifteen minutes every hour!"

"No, my friend. I didn't cheat," came the reply. "All I did was stop to sharpen my axe."

This story reminds us of the importance of tending to our own tools. In the case of legacy building, this means taking care of yourself. Self-compassion is where you show yourself the same kindness and understanding that you would give a friend if they were suffering or struggling.

Once you love yourself, you can love those around you in the very best way before you try to teach them. This is how you prepare them the way a farmer would prepare the land. In this chapter I encourage you to sharpen your axe by stopping for a moment, considering the lessons, and then going back to swinging.

Having Impact

Some people believe that our society is divided into ladder people and rope people. Let's say you're walking down a road and you see a huge hole. As you get closer, you realize that there are people in the hole, and when they see you, they start yelling for help to get out. Ladder people hand down a ladder and let those people crawl out of the hole on their own. Rope people throw them a rope and pull them up themselves.

Both ladders and ropes get people out of the holes, but the difference is one wants to give the people in need a resource they need to climb out of the hole on their own, while the other asks them to do little more than hold on. When this happens, the rope person gets to decide how far and how fast to pull. The rope doesn't give the power back to the person in the hole.

You've probably heard that common saying, "Give a man a fish, and you feed him for a day. Teach a man to fish, and you feed him for a lifetime." It might be a little cliché at this point, but the meaning is still powerful. Being the help that actually helps is the goal of making an impact on the world, which is what leaving a legacy is all about.

When I say impact the world, I mean each of the rings in the diagram at the start of this section. The world starts with you and then expands to include those closest people in your life. Once you have made an impact there, it moves to the world around you, starting with your local community and moving out to include anyone you have the potential to reach through the world and in the future.

I want to start with you—the individual. Legacies start with just one person. For my family it started with Grandpa Ken and GG. They were the kind of people who loved themselves and loved their families first. They took care of each other and us, and then they looked outward to see how they could be of service outside the home. When they saw that a need existed in our little hometown of Buttonwillow for a church, they went and built one. This was an example that my generation and I watched and followed, so when we saw a need in our hometown for a church, we helped build one too.

You'll know you've made an impact when your life is full. For me personally, I notice my life is full when my family is all together. Family support has always been a part of my life. I remember the first time I played soccer. I don't remember how old I was, but I couldn't have been more than seven or eight. But I do clearly remember my dad and my uncle were my coaches.

I'll never forget the first goal I scored. I turned around and saw my grandpa and my dad and my uncle jumping up and down. They were all so proud of me. I'm fifty now, and I still have goose bumps remembering how that made me feel.

That constant support has been passed down in my family through all these years. Even today my dad goes to every single one of his grandkids' games. It doesn't matter if it is three hours away or fifteen minutes away, he is there. We've been in business meetings at work, and my dad gets up in the middle of everything and just leaves. I'll ask, "Where are you going?"

"Halle's got a volleyball game," he'll remind me as he walks out the door. Halle is my daughter, but he does this for all of his grandkids.

Legacy building starts with family.

But then it takes looking beyond just friends and family. I believe it is important to start with your local circles first, because that is where you have the greatest opportunities to see needs and fill them in meaningful ways. For us that next circle begins with our employees— as they are just extended family in our eyes.

The Wegis/Young legacy is being built every day using this principle. A number of years ago, my cousin Greg wanted to do something meaningful for the employees that work in the field day after day on behalf of our family. He suggested we start a scholarship fund for the benefit of children of employees of the company who want to attend college. Many children of farm workers are the first in their generation to attend college. We have been blessed as a family to be able to give to the children of employees that have given so much.

Legacy building also takes courage. You've probably come across that famous Winston Churchill quote: "Courage is going from failure to failure without losing enthusiasm." I love this one so much. My grandfather always believed he was always better off taking a chance while accepting the risk of failure. This is a great balance between my dad and uncle Rick as well, when it comes to business. They take calculated risks with a clear hope for the future.

Legacy building isn't passive. It is an active, intentional effort to do things that will live on after you are gone. I hope you have the moral courage to do the right thing and the civic courage to actually do it. I have given you just a few examples of how impact can have a ripple effect. It's all about looking in and then looking out. I always say self-change plus loving relationships equals impact.

SELF CHANGE + LOVING RELATIONSHIPS = *impact*

Building Relationships

When my dad was in training for Vietnam, he looked for ways to build relationships despite the very real risk that his buddies would be shipped out to different places and possibly never come home. His closest friend, Michael (the person I am named after), invested in a friendship that gave them both strength, despite the circumstances. It would have been so easy for either of them to pull inward and refuse to connect out of self-preservation, but they didn't. Friendship was important.

After being deployed, Dad said, "Michael and I were in the same place, but he was in a different company once we got to Vietnam, so I didn't see him much once we were deployed. But the guys I was with truly became my band of brothers. It just happens when you are at war. You are bonded in a brotherhood. They might not be your friends, but there's something there that binds. Something thicker than blood."

These relationships were everything to those young soldiers, and they remained brothers for the rest of their lives.

I want to encourage you to sharpen your axe by considering what is keeping you from building the kind of relationships you deserve. Then find ways to connect with others that aren't just your family. This is risky. I get it. You might get hurt or rejected or taken advantage of. But it's no more risky than those soldiers at war. And in a sense, we are all at war, aren't we? We are fighting the enemies of loneliness, depression, anxiety, apathy, and all those isolating factors that keep us apart. Find your band of brothers and sisters, and build a web of friends and colleagues who support you and whom you can support. No one has ever thrived in a vacuum.

There is an incredible TED Talk by researcher Elizabeth Lesser called "Take 'the Other' to Lunch."[21] She recommends looking for people who are different from us and then intentionally spending time getting to know them. I suggest the same thing. Identify one person you normally would not have considered building a relationship with, and give them a chance to tell you who they are and what they believe. You will very likely be surprised how much value they can add to your life.

This is your chance to expand your network beyond your current circle. I'm guessing if you were to write down everyone in your network, you'd have family, friends, old schoolmates, coworkers, colleagues, maybe some people from church or other organizations you belong to. Try expanding that to include people from other walks of life. Join a book club or a civic organization. Run for office or volunteer. Become a mentor!

In their book *The Compound Effect*, author Darren Hardy uses the term "reference group" to include everyone you regularly come in contact with. Their research shows that this group can determine "as much as 95 percent of your success or failure in life."[22]

To simplify this, the principle is that if you want to be more successful, start hanging out with more successful people. The beauty is that there is no cap to how many people you can include. Your

---

21   Elizabeth Lesser, "Take 'the Other' to lunch," TED, accessed June 6, 2023, https://www.ted.com/talks/elizabeth_lesser_take_the_other_to_lunch.

22   Darren Hardy, *The Compound Effect* (Bhopal, India: Manjul Publishing, 2021).

reference group can and should be constantly expanding throughout your life. My mother and my cousin Jane are the masters of this. They lead with an inquisitive heart in all they do and toward all they meet. They are open and friendly to everyone and truly want to learn about others. One person leads to another, and before you know it, they have a circle that is as large as our hometown. It's hard to go somewhere with my mother or Jane and not run into someone they know. It is the curiosity that they carry with them everywhere that keeps their circles fresh and wide.

It's been said that we all become the average of our closest ten people. When you look at the health, financial stability, happiness, and lifestyle of your ten closest people, are you content with being the average of them? If not, you can cultivate new relationships to shift that center so it lies closer to your goals.

I want to remind you that building relationships is also about generosity. As you build existing relationships and create new ones, don't be stingy with your time or your money. As I like to say, share your time, talent, and treasure. When you do, you will see it returned in multiples.

Moving Fearlessly

How many people today go through life on autopilot? It's like they are driving down a freeway at rush hour, sitting numbly in their cars with the radio on, not paying attention to anything past the car ahead of them. They go through life this way, not even realizing that there are other options.

Some people do realize they are in constant gridlock and raise their eyes to look beyond. They step out of the car and suddenly realize that they have far more control over their journey. They have greater flexibility in choosing where they end up because they are using their own two feet rather than sitting in a traffic jam going where everyone else is going. They may eventually end up at the same place they were going before, but the experience of getting there is different. Better. They are able to change directions more easily and try things during the journey that they couldn't before.

Now is time to take intentional action and begin establishing a microculture around you that you can be proud of. You can create the world you want to see. There's no time like the present, as they say. Remember, goals are accomplished in small steps.

Servant Leadership

I was born into a family with strong women. My grandmother, my mother, and my aunt are the real muscles behind the strength of our family. But more than muscle, they are servant leaders. The legacy they passed to the next generation is that we found spouses that are servant leaders themselves.

In my observation some of the best examples of what it means to be a servant leader can be found in new mothers. A servant leader is someone who puts others' needs before their own and is willing to go out of their way to help those around them. New mothers are constantly putting their own needs aside to care for their newborn babies.

A new mother is willing to sacrifice her own sleep and comfort to ensure that her baby is safe and healthy. A new mother is constantly monitoring her baby's needs and making sure they are being met. A new mother is willing to go out of her way to make sure that her baby is comfortable and happy, even at the sacrifice of her own comfort. I have heard it said, "Mother and baby cannot be comfortable at the same time." This seems to be the case as so many young mothers push their physical and mental limits on behalf of their infant.

This was exemplified with how my wife, Jenn, mothered all our children, but especially our youngest, Jacob. Jacob was born with a clubfoot, a congenital malformation where his foot was rotated inward and downward. One thing we knew was that we didn't want to start the path of major surgery with a newborn. Jenn tirelessly researched the condition. This was before the time of Doctor Google, so you can imagine how easy it was with three children under the age of six.

She took weekly six-hour round trips to an orthopedic expert who was willing to treat Jacob's foot in a manner that was noninvasive. While it did require a few minor surgeries, Jenn's persistent servant leadership over the course of six years got Jacob's foot to a place where it was nearly normal.

You see, a new mother is a servant leader in the way that she is willing to be patient and understanding so that she can understand her baby's needs without having to have them explicitly communicated in words. She is a servant leader in the way that she is willing to go out of her way to make sure that her baby is taken care of. She is willing to take on extra tasks and responsibilities to ensure that her baby has everything they need. And she is willing to put her own needs aside to make sure that her baby is safe and healthy.

If you want to be a servant leader, start by doing one simple thing that is, perhaps, inconvenient for you. Jesus didn't start by washing the feet of his disciples. He first learned their names. Then he invited them to come and walk with him. He was generous with his time. I'm sure that there were many long conversations as they walked those dusty roads between one town and the next. Eventually, they were so close that when he did bow at their feet with a basin of water, they were not freaked out. They understood his intent and allowed themselves to be touched in such an intimate, humble way.

Servant leaders put others before themselves.

Obligation to Serve

There is a famous Spider-Man quote, "With great power comes great responsibility." I smile at this because most people don't realize that it actually comes from the Bible. It's really just another way of saying, "Everyone to whom much was given, of him much will be required, and from him to whom they entrusted much, they will demand the more" (Luke 12:48 ESV).

I am so thankful that I was born here in America. I don't think we talk enough about how special it is to live here. We have so many advantages and blessings that we take for granted. If we are going to "walk the walk," we have an obligation to leave a legacy greater than what was handed to us.

I believe that everybody has something to offer, and to leave and live a legacy, you must love sacrificially and pour life into those around you. Societies throughout the history of the world make progress because of human potential. For most of human history, there was this controlling view of humanity where only a small amount of people made the decisions for the masses. Think of how civilization advanced from the Roman Empire to the Dark Ages to the Renaissance. For centuries the typical person just struggled to survive in all of these eras.

But then in 1776, a more expansive view of human potential came about—the Declaration of Independence. The Declaration of Independence was a huge bet on people. It bet that every individual had something to contribute to make progress in ways that that would be beneficial for everyone else individually. That philosophy allowed humanity to rise together. That is the American experiment. It is what makes the United States the greatest country in the world to live in.

Unfortunately, these principles were not evenly applied and practiced right out of the gates. They excluded African Americans, Native Americans, and women. But our history has been a steady march of expanding the definition of an "individual." This means we have been making a bigger bet on more and more people. Whether it is the abolition of slavery, the inclusion of women in terms of voting rights, the civil rights movement, or the increasing welcoming of more immigrants from the far reaches of the world, our country has offered individuals more rights and more opportunities to contribute with the passage of time, and that's something we can be proud of.

In each case of expansion, a few brave souls fought against long odds at great personal risk to themselves to leave a legacy, because they had the moral courage to act. There are hundreds and thousands of stories of individuals who would've been written off in different parts of history, but instead, because we bet on them, we are all better off. Because of them, our nation has a greater diversity of ideas and the greater probability of breakthrough innovations and true progress.

There is no doubt that this great American experiment has paid incredible dividends, be it by economic prosperity, longevity, or opportunity. We owe that progress to the core fundamental belief that our founding fathers had, in that everyone has something to contribute. If everyone has something to offer, then let's bet on them. It's our turn to build on that legacy that has been handed to us. A bet on humanity is a vital part of the code.

Citizenship fuels the flames of unity, binding generations together in a shared legacy. It empowers individuals to shape their nation's destiny, leaving behind a lasting imprint on the tapestry of history. To live the Code is to be an active and productive citizen in your community.

I know this is a really big chapter in terms of the concepts I have discussed. As you continue to build your legacy in earnest, I want to remind you that each of these steps is crucial: adequate preparation of yourself and others, considering the impact you want to make and then being intentional toward that goal, working to build mutually beneficial relationships, and moving with courage toward becoming a servant leader.

You before me is a key piece to the farmer's code.

you > me

Strengthening

The Farmer's Code

There are few professions in the world that require as much resilience as that of the farmer. Farmers are constantly susceptible to the threats of unpredictable weather patterns, pest outbreaks, technology failures, and market fluctuations, among other things. If farmers weren't resilient, this world would be a very hungry place indeed.

A farmer's strength to overcome starts with the qualities of courage, integrity, and adaptability in the face of challenges. To leave a legacy, we must also have the courage and integrity to persevere through difficult times and the ability to adapt and change to grow and develop as a person.

Courage

We all know people who seem to live on autopilot. It's like they are driving down the freeway of life, letting the flow of traffic take them numbly from one place to another. The radio is blaring, and they don't bother to try and see anything past the vehicles right next to them. They could be on the moon for all they notice.

And then there are the people who lift their heads and realize at some point that traffic is actually not taking them where they want to go. They realize their purpose isn't to be on a never-ending road of sameness, so they pull over and step out of the car. They realize that if they stop driving and start walking, they suddenly have control over their journey. Sure, it's harder than being on autopilot, but that effort gives them a great amount of freedom and flexibility. Of course, they may end up at the same place that they would have before, but by having the courage to take each step intentionally, there is value to that destination.

Take a second to ponder if you like the destination or the journey better. Do you spend your life always thinking about where you're going and when you're going to get there? Or do you take the time and enjoy the steps that come between? It's like a child in a car repeating, "Are we there yet?" and missing the marvels out their window.

By having the courage to turn off the autopilot and take a step off the common path, you can see things you never would have seen and try things you never would have tried. There is a satisfaction at the end of this journey, but there is also joy in the journey itself.

Integrity

A common definition of integrity is doing the right thing when nobody else is watching. I like this, but I don't think it's quite complete. Integrity is not only doing the right thing when nobody is watching—it's doing what you are supposed to be doing. What you came to earth to do.

Our lives have significance. It is human nature to want to help others. Through God we can understand when to come to the rescue of others and when to allow them to help themselves. Sometimes, the most compassionate thing we can do is allow others to struggle, thereby learning the lessons they need to learn. For a parent this is an enormous challenge. You never want to see your child hurt or grieving. But if we prevent them from experiencing the challenges of life, we also prevent them from being strengthened in the way they need to endure the next trial that will inevitably come. Integrity can look like following God's plan before your own. This way we can be the help that actually helps.

In Luke chapter 10, we learn that when we trust wholeheartedly in the Lord, we can better serve those around us. "Love your neighbor as yourself." Honestly, this is one of the most difficult things asked of us in the Bible. But it's a universal theme in nearly every religion and philosophy. In more secular circles, it's called the Golden Rule. It's in the Torah—"Love your neighbor as yourself" (Leviticus 19:18), the Qur'an—"Do good to parents, kinsfolk, orphans, those in need, neighbors who are near, neighbors who are strangers, the companion by your side, the wayfarer ..." (Mahabharata 5,1517), and in Hindu writings—"This is the sum of duty/do naught unto others what you would not have them do unto you." Love and compassion for all people are foundational to Buddhist and Baha'i teachings. In fact you'd be hard pressed to find many spiritual teachings that don't include this basic guidance.

The way I interpret this is it is our responsibility to help those in need, regardless of a person's past or present situation. It isn't our job to judge them in any way; we only are asked to help. This can often be hard when it seems to us our help isn't deserved. If you can tolerate someone's weaknesses, there is no reason you can't be friends with them. Too often the weaknesses are far more visible than the strengths of strangers, and we must try to look past those and be willing to befriend people regardless. Revelation requires responsibility and integrity.

I'm going to tell a little story to help illustrate this. Imagine you are perched on a narrow fence, living without any desire or knowledge about how to get down. You are visited by two birds, one prompting you to climb the ladder on the right and one prompting you to go down on the left. You decide to climb down on the right. As soon as your feet hit the ground, the ladders on either side disappear. Now you realize there is no way to get back on the fence.

This fence can be related to our lives. While sitting on the fence, we are living in ignorance, not knowing there is a choice that needs to be made. As soon as we are prompted to move, we climb off that fence and must make the choice to follow what the Lord asks us to do or not. There is no middle ground; we must either be on the Lord's side or not. Through revelation we have a responsibility to act. This can be frightening. We know once we accept the Lord, he will not only change our own life, but He will also use us to change many others.

Greg said, "Grandma Vivian has had an incredible influence on the fourth and fifth generations, from the way she lived and continues to live life. She has a sense of calmness that comes from always living her life for love of family and friends, honesty, hard work, focus, purpose, and her relationship with God. I've never seen her deviate from any of these principles that she lives her life by, and it is infectious within the family."

Adaptability

When my daughter Halle turned nine, all she wanted was a turtle. She said she was ready for the responsibility of taking care of a pet after becoming obsessed with sea turtles while on a vacation to the Florida coast. You can imagine the anticipation of a little girl about to get her own pet.

When we got to the pet store, the first turtle she saw was the one we brought home. They put him in a box, and we were on our way. On the way home, Halle wanted everyone's opinions on what we should name him. Many names bounced around the car, but nothing stuck.

The turtle did not like the box and kept scratching and scratching at it, trying to find a way out. I said we should name him "Scratch." Of course that was a dumb idea until the next day, when it wasn't.

Scratch was a part of our family for many years. What I loved about watching Scratch was that he only made progress when he stuck his head out, but he always knew when to pull his neck in. You see, Scratch was the ultimate metaphor for legacy living. You must know when to retreat and when to admit mistakes. You must also know when to be vulnerable enough to stick your neck out and look ahead and how to swivel to see new perspectives.

As I mentioned in the beginning, I can't think of many professions in the world that require more resilience than that of a farmer, but I think the role of a spouse is right up there. My dad said, "I'd say if anyone can live through the first year of marriage, there'd be no reason for a divorce, ever." Obviously, many people live happily for a few years before things fall apart, but the sentiment is true. If you can stick with it through that difficult first year when you're learning so much about each other, you should have enough faith in yourself and your spouse that you can make it through anything else that comes.

We should be like water. Rivers are one of nature's strongest forces. They are drawn to the sea, and no matter the obstacles, they always eventually reach it, even if that means taking centuries to cut through solid rock. Rivers adapt; they constantly find and change paths.

My sister-in-law Melissa tells a story about my nephew Aiden. He was really excited to be a part of the associated student body (ASB) and wanted to be president of his class. He ran for that office many years in a row, but every year he lost. To him this didn't matter. He went and tried again. My daughter Emma had run for different ASB positions and lost, too, and she could have discouraged him because she never won either. But she didn't. She and the rest of the family supported him. At family gatherings we would say things like, "Well, you're a Young. You're going to lose. And that's just how this goes!"

He tried for many years and didn't give up. And every time the family was like, "Well, one day you will break that Young tradition of losing!"

And he finally did. That's the way we do things in this family. We try things, and even if we fail the first time, or twenty times, we always try again until we get it right.

The term "pivot" is often used to indicate flexibility and resilience. It was quite the buzzword coming out of the COVID-19 pandemic. This reminds me of the Greek myth about King Sisyphus, who was cursed by Zeus to roll a massive boulder up a hill for all eternity. As soon as he got within a few feet of the top, the boulder would break loose and roll to the bottom. Everybody has a giant boulder in their lives. Sometimes many of them. But we don't have to be like Sisyphus. Once we get them moving, we are able to keep pushing them up and over the top. The key is to figure out how to adapt and to never give up. Even when things seem to get a little easier, we have to keep working just as hard as when things are challenging. Winston Churchill famously said, "Never give in, never give in, never, never, never, never—in nothing, great or small, large or petty—never give in except to convictions of honor and good sense."

I think it's just about impossible to be resilient without adaptability. This is how you strengthen yourself and your legacy.

Keep the Right Perspective

You must be optimistic to put a seed in the ground and hope that it will provide for the future of your family. Being positive doesn't mean you are happy all the time. It means that even on the hard days, you know that better ones are coming.

As I wrote earlier in the book, I recently ruptured my Achilles tendon playing pickleball, of all things. Yes, in all of my endurance endeavors, it was pickleball that took me down. And while I was suffering physically, there were times that I was really suffering mentally. For a guy who is the master of multitasking and doesn't sit still well, the thought of six to eight months of recovery in a cast and being immobile really took a toll. But I have a great friend, Jim Damian, who had some sage advice. Jim is bigger than life. Physically, he is bigger than me. But Jim is also a guy that lights up every room he steps into and is the life of the party. He is witty, a talker, a great family man, an amazing CEO, and an even better friend. Jim is one of the most optimistic people I know.

You wouldn't know it to look at him, but Jim has really dealt with adversity. A few years ago, Jim was at the dentist for a routine cleaning. The dental hygienist found a small bump on the inside of his mouth. That bump turned into some major surgeries where a quarter of his jaw was removed. He then had his jaw wired shut for over five months for the recovery. For a man that loves to talk and eat, you would think this would be a tragedy. But Jim was a champ and embraced the situation with pure optimism. That isn't to say he never got angry, sad, or even depressed at the situation. Some days just sucked. But you wouldn't know how down he was when you saw him, because Jim is always optimistic. He understood this was just a blip in time for him.

A few days after I went down with my Achilles injury, Jim called. He said, "I know you are anxious—probably more than you've ever been in your life. And I know you are trying to hold it together and you can't. I know you probably feel like you are going a bit crazy. You're not. I was there. Just know that the anxiety will fade and be replaced by acceptance in a few weeks. Heck, in three weeks you'll be wondering why you even need two legs. In a month you'll start having days where you hardly think about it. It is what it is. Use this terrible, beautiful, sickening sweet time as an opportunity for growth."

Now, how is that for optimism? That conversation carried me through my recovery.

We have a familiar story that we tell around the dinner table sometimes about our grandparents. My cousin Greg tells it best:

> *My grandparents had some friends that were farmers also. We grew up down the street from them. One year they did well. I think it was a good cotton year, and they decided to buy a beach house on Padaro Lane, outside of Santa Barbara. There was another house for sale for $100,000 or $120,000, and my grandfather's friend told him he should buy it. But Grandpa thought it was a bad investment. He thought it was better to*

invest the money in a motor home so he didn't have to keep a house just in one place. He wanted to be able to go where he wanted. So, he bought a motor home (a depreciating asset), and I think it was worth $20,000 when he sold it. If he had bought that beach house, it would now be worth somewhere like $15 million. But to be fair, we spent a lot of good family times in that motor home. We went on a lot of road trips and had a lot of happy memories playing cards and just traveling with my grandparents. So, it wasn't that bad of an investment when you look at the family history and how much time we spent together. I wouldn't trade those memories for anything.

My brother Jeff added, "They called it the Wiggie Wagon. Grandma and Grandpa always made a point to spend a lot of time with their grandkids. We'd travel all over the place. They took us everywhere. Those trips in that motor home were some of the best vacations we had."

I want to acknowledge that optimism is great, but life is not always sunshine and roses as we learned from my friend Jim Damian. If you are familiar with the Vietnam War, you might know that Admiral Jim Stockdale was the highest-ranking American military officer held in the infamous Hanoi Hilton. He survived for seven-and-a-half years there as a prisoner of war. This place was about as close to hell as anyone could ever experience on earth. After his release he shared what he had come to call "the Stockdale Paradox." He observed in his time there that the POWs who survived were those who found a balance between reality and optimism, not pure optimists. The way he told it was that optimists would, for example, convince themselves that they would be out by Christmas. Christmas would come and go, and so they would decide they'd be home by Easter. Then they would shift their goal to Thanksgiving, followed by another Christmas. "And then they died of a broken heart," he said. Pure optimism without a dose of reality did not give them long-lasting resilience.

He told new prisoners, "You must never confuse faith that you will prevail in the end—which you can never afford to lose—with the discipline to confront the most brutal facts of your current reality, whatever they might be. We are not getting out by Christmas. Deal with it." In this way, prisoners would find ways to make the reality bearable.

WE WANT TO BE SUCCESSFUL, TO BE HAPPY, AND TO ACHIEVE SOMETHING OF SIGNIFICANCE. BUT SIMPLE POSITIVE VISUALIZATION WILL NOT GET US THESE THINGS.

After they did finally return home, he said, "I never doubted not only that I would get out, but also that I would prevail in the end and turn the experience into the defining event of my life, which, in retrospect, I would not trade."[23]

We all want things to work out for the best. We want to be successful, to be happy, and to achieve something of significance. But simple positive visualization will not get us these things. Thinking happy thoughts makes us feel nice, but this has to be counterbalanced with reality.

To leave a legacy of good, you can't always care about what others think of you or what you do. It is important to treat others well, even when no one is looking. You are only as good a person as who you are when there's no one around you. We should strive to be the same regardless of who is there. There is a phenomenon in psychology called

23   Jim and Sybil Stockdale, *In Love & War: The Story of a Family's Ordeal and Sacrifice during the Vietnam Years* (New York: Harper & Row, 1984).

the bystander effect. This states that despite common sense, people in crowds often don't receive the needed support. This is because those who see it happen will often think to themselves that it's someone else's problem to help. They justify not helping because there are so many other people who could also help. This thought process is not beneficial. One thing to always try and live by is when you see a need, fill that need. We can try to justify our actions, but, in the end, there is truly no right way to do the wrong things. Keeping the right perspective, being adaptable in most situations while having courage and integrity in all that you do are key components of the farmer's code.

fourteen

Marketing

The Farmer's Code

Farmers don't tend to be visible to the general public. For the most part, we're fairly content to keep our heads down and do our jobs without fanfare. The market for modern fresh produce has origins that trace back to when human beings developed a taste for cultivated food like apples, lettuce, and nuts. Because of this we typically don't have to make much ado about our products in order to sell them. Our buyers come to us looking to fill long-established demands.

We've grown used to slogans like "I'm lovin' it," "Finger lickin' good," "They're gr-r-reat!" or "Eat fresh." They are so ubiquitous that we almost don't even notice them anymore. Have you ever stopped to think about all the items in the grocery store that don't have slogans or marketing campaigns? Can you imagine the phrases that would fill the produce section of the grocery store if farmers had to try to market all of their crops? "Almonds: The Little Nut that Could!" "Orange You Glad You Like Carrots?" "You're the Avocado to My Toast." Or "Strawberries—Because Chocolate Can't Do All the Heavy Lifting."

We don't need slogans to prompt us to buy fresh produce, because people know the inherent value of fruits, veggies, legumes, nuts, and so on. I suppose one could say that is the "brand" of our products.

The phrase "personal brand" started to creep into business and self-help discussions in the late '90s and slowly seeped into the common vernacular over the next couple of decades. It is the topic of countless articles, webinars, books, retreats, and life coach curricula. They all pretty much say the same thing: your personal brand is something that is developed over time, just like a farmer's produce. It is based on how you interact with the world.

Legacies, like a farmer's product and your personal brand, require care, attention, and positive promotion in order to live beyond the "farm stand."

Character Is Brand

Today, we often use the term "brand" in place of the words "personality," "reputation," or "identity." In the end, it's all the same. Personal "brand" refers to the image and perception that an individual presents to the world based on their unique combination of skills, strengths, experiences, values, and personality traits. Your brand distinguishes you from others and is the basis of your distinct and memorable identity. It is what makes you stand out, builds a loyal following, and establishes you as an expert or thought leader.

But here's the thing. Most people believe that they can dictate and control what their brand is in the world. They are wrong. Because your brand is founded on the perception you have through the eyes of others, society gets to determine what it is. The way you treat others, the things you say and do, and your attitude are all factors that go into that brand, but you have zero control over how others react to you. You can't control what they do with the impressions you make on them any more than you can force people to like you. The best you can do is be as authentic to who you really are as you possibly can and let that do the work. Like mangoes or peppers sitting in a pile in the produce section, you are just one of the bunch. Shine the best way you can, and let the world see how great you are deep inside.

There is so much more to our identity than what is seen on the outside. If you search the name Reverend Joel Hawes on the internet, you'll find that he was the minister at the First Congregational Church in Hartford, Connecticut, at the turn of the nineteenth century. You'll also likely find that he was best known for his published sermons and other writings, in particular a series of lectures he gave in 1827 in an effort to address the spiritual dangers he knew young men faced in that day. His most famous quote from those lectures says, "A good character is, in all cases, the fruit of personal exertion. It is not inherited from parents; it is not created by external advantages; it is no necessary appendage of birth, wealth, talents, or station; but it is the result of one's own endeavors—the fruit and reward of good principles manifested in a course of virtuous and honorable action."

My family is full of people who have never heard the word "brand" in this context, and they certainly never gave a second thought to what the world thought of them. My cousin Greg said, "Our grandfathers and great-grandfathers were some of the hardest working people in the world. Just grinders out in the dirt and the heat. We always look at them as setting the foundation for what we've been able to build on. It wasn't the easiest life." They just did what they did and did it as well as they could. If the world didn't like it, that was of no consequence.

Their hard work had more to do with character than effort. Pure effort alone just leads to quick exhaustion, and there often comes a point where you can't continue. Think about the story of the tortoise and the hare. If you haven't read this children's story in a while, the two main characters are a tortoise and a hare. They decide to have a race, which everyone thinks is absurd, but the tortoise is determined to show the hare he can win. The race starts, and the hare quickly dashes off the start line. Meanwhile, the tortoise moves at a slower pace but is consistent in his efforts. After quite a bit of running, the hare finds himself tired. He looks behind him, and with no tortoise in sight, he decides that he is so far ahead he can rest here for a while and still win. Soon after lying down, the hare falls asleep. The hare dreams lazily, and the tortoise never quits. He keeps moving, and before long he passes the hare. When the hare finally awakens, he quickly dashes to the finish line. Much to his surprise, the tortoise has already crossed it, proving his claim that "slow and steady wins the race."

Both characters in this story are true to their nature, or "brands," if you will. The hare being quick to move and quick to tire. The tortoise being determined and steady. And in this case, the brand of the tortoise proved most successful.

It is important to know your strengths and weaknesses as you progress and work to better yourself. As stated throughout this book, self-awareness allows you to understand what things you do well and how to use those to your advantage. Knowing your weaknesses, which is arguably harder for many people, is just as important. As you come to know what your weaknesses are, you can strengthen them and progress in a beneficial way. The better you get at recognizing and addressing your shortcomings, the easier it will become. Like any other skill, this can be improved through practice.

The best way to get better is to learn by doing. It's like a brain sport. As you do it more, you begin to develop needed muscle memory. Father Richard Rohr is an American Franciscan priest, and I believe him to be one of the foremost thought leaders on what it means to be your "true self." Father Rohr describes how within us all there is a true self, which is your eternal essence, and a false self, which he calls your shadow. While the shadow self is the persona that you created, Rohr instructs us to dig into our shadow so that our true essence can shine.

Choose Role Models Wisely

As you are developing your personal brand, having an example to follow really helps. For most of my family, GG is the ideal role model. She has been the ideal example of love, respect, hard work, and strength.

"Growing up, Grandma Vivian was the only girl in her family with a bunch of brothers," my brother shared. "She was always tough as nails. The one thing she loved—and we loved trying to challenge her on—was arm wrestling. She's this little five-foot-nothing, less-than-a-hundred-pound grandma, but I don't think any of us could beat her until we got into high school. I mean, she was very strong. If you ask any of the boys in the family, I guarantee they will all agree that we've arm wrestled Grandma more than we've arm wrestled anyone else in our life."

When I asked her about her memory of this, GG laughed and said, "If you can beat them in arm wrestling, then I think they better darn well listen to you, right?"

Having positive role models at an early age can help young people develop a sense of purpose, self-confidence, and a strong work ethic. They can also help individuals to learn important life skills, such as communication, leadership, and problem-solving. Learning to do something alone can often be hard. Ultimately, role models are important because they provide inspiration, guidance, and motivation for us as we work to achieve our goals and aspirations. They can be anyone with the qualities, values, or achievements that we admire and want to emulate, including parents, teachers, celebrities, or even fictional characters.

Mark Nepo wrote in his book *Surviving Storms: Finding the Strength to Meet Adversity,* "Admiration is a powerful resource because when we admire someone or something, we are, if open, introduced to where those qualities live in us. Then, it is our work to stay in conversation with those qualities, to discern how to water them and nurture them. It is our work to let those qualities of admiration grow from within us out into the world."[24]

I have admiration for many different people and many different things. I admire them because they inherently have qualities that I want to carry in my life. I admire my dog Chloe as she loves without hesitation. But I don't want to be my dog. I admire the faith and resilience of professional surfer Bethany Hamilton, who lost her arm to a shark but continued to be one of the best in the world at her craft. But I don't want to be Bethany. I admire Richard Branson, CEO of Virgin Group, and his growth mindset while doing what he wants in life without worrying about what other people think. But I don't want to be Richard Branson.

I take note of the things I admire and try to integrate those qualities into my life, but not to the point where I lose myself. And

---

24   Mark Nepo, *Surviving Storms: Finding the Strength to Meet Adversity* (New York: St. Martin's Essentials, 2022).

as I learn more about great people and why they do what they do, I can look a little deeper into myself to figure out why I do what I do. As my grandparents taught, be yourself, and let the world decide for itself what to make of you.

The right role models can also provide a sense of community and belonging, especially for individuals who may not have strong support networks in their personal lives. By observing and learning from role models, we can become more successful, productive, and fulfilled in our personal and professional lives. I challenge you to become a student of admiration. What do you admire about the people, things, and animals around you? Where do you see "awe" in the world? How do these qualities mirror your own possibility of living life to the fullest?

> I TAKE NOTE OF THE THINGS I ADMIRE AND TRY TO INTEGRATE THOSE QUALITIES INTO MY LIFE, BUT NOT TO THE POINT WHERE I LOSE MYSELF.

Family Before Business

Priorities are another key aspect of personal branding. In our family, respect is the number one priority and the key to our success. Running a business as a family has its challenges, but through respectful communication, it is possible. Family trumps everything else, no matter what.

"I see us as just a family that happens to do business," said Gina. "Not really a family business. There are so many multigenerational businesses out there. I think the passion for making a true family that does business is what makes us so special. We are going to do whatever it takes to put the family first. This family really respects each other, which is really unique because in other family businesses, it can be a soap opera."

As businesses grow there will inevitably be issues, but by being vulnerable, willing to communicate, and respecting everyone, it is possible to excel. By focusing on family first, working through company issues runs a lot smoother. One of the keys to making family a priority is vulnerability. Vulnerability is key. When each member of the family is able to share their authentic story, the fabric of our relationships bonds tighter and stronger. My grandparents were so young when they got married. This could have worked against them, as we see in so many marriages where young people grow apart. Instead, they took the opportunity to create a family dynamic that put each other first. GG said of her marriage, "We put each other first. We were so young when we got married that we always said we raised each other."

This was evident in the way they raised their children. My mom said, "My parents always believed in fun, and that's how I believe. I think if you're going to work together, you have to be able to play together. And if you can't play together, something falls apart. And of course there is lots of love, which is the core to everything. My parents were always a good team."

Be Intentional

Being intentional in all that you do is an important life lesson to learn. It means to be mindful and aware of the things you do and the decisions you make. Intentionality leads to clarity and focus in life, allowing you to be more productive and successful. It helps to keep you motivated and allows you to be more creative and innovative in your pursuits. It also encourages personal growth, since it requires you to be mindful of your thoughts, feelings, and actions. Ultimately, being intentional in all that you do allows you to live a life of purpose and fulfillment, which leads to a legacy well beyond you.

A group of friends and I had the opportunity to visit the naval amphibious base in Coronado, California, a few years back. It is home to naval special warfare command as well as SEAL teams one, three, five, and seven. The US Navy SEAL program is famous for telling its recruits to "get comfortable with being uncomfortable." This is wise advice for one who is working on themselves and trying to improve from the inside out. This means we must stop being incidental and start being intentional.

We all know that we have a limited amount of time on Earth. Time is our most precious commodity and something that we will never get back. Life is meant to be lived to the fullest and not squandered. When our oldest child, Emma, finished sixth grade, the concept of time smacked Jenn and me upside the face. Jenn woke up one morning and realized we only had six summers left before Emma left for college, at which point we would no longer control her schedule. Six summers—think about that. We only had six more chances to show the world to the family when we were still all together.

So, that began a time of travel. We took every opportunity we had in those six years leading up to Emma leaving for college to show our children the world. Summer vacations, Christmas vacations, and spring breaks were spent as a family discovering new cultures and visiting places we'd never been. It really instilled the wanderlust value in our kids. Time is precious; living it intentionally makes it much more sweet.

Leaving a legacy isn't about the "things" you leave behind. Rather, it is about how you work to shape the future. As you intentionally work toward leaving a legacy, you must remember it is the small things you do every day that make up who you are. Keep in mind what message you want to send to people, and act accordingly in every space you are in.

Never Give Up

Life can be pretty hard sometimes. It pushes you around, flipping you this way and that. You get thrown on the ground, then picked up just to be knocked down again. However, there is a lot of joy to be found in life. It is our responsibility to live life intentionally and take in all that it has to offer. To soak it up.

Bruce Lee said, "Effort is the path of man to mastery." When I thought about the legacy my grandpa Ken left and what he taught me about growth, there were a number of things that came to mind. He put a lot of effort into everything he did. He was not the kind of man who would stop partway through a project. If it meant staying up long past the sun went down, so be it. The job had to be done before he would quit.

I also learned from him to celebrate the wins. When I was a freshman in college, he took a group of us on a fishing trip to Alaska. This was a big deal to him. He paid for the whole trip and had us staying in a great lodge and fishing for five days straight. We fished for king salmon on the Nushagak River, and we fished for halibut in the wild waters of the Pacific Ocean.

For four days he didn't catch a single fish. But we kept going out. On the last day, we were out on the ocean, and everyone else in the group was reeling in halibut all day long. Everyone except Grandpa. He still couldn't catch a thing. At the end of the day, the boat captain told us to start taking in our lines. As we started to pull them in, Grandpa clearly had something. His reel was spinning out of control so vigorously that they thought there was a shark on the line. Everyone was excited, getting ready for this shark. One of the crew said it had to be a great white.

When the fish finally surfaced, to everyone's surprise it was a huge king salmon. All the men on the boat said, "We have never seen a king salmon that big get hooked on a halibut line!" The fish was so big that it took Jeff, Greg, and me to hold it up for the photo.

It was literally the last fish that we caught on the whole trip. Everyone was super successful except Grandpa. Even though he caught this gigantic fish at the last minute, I'll never forget what he said. "Michael, you know good things don't always come to those who wait."

I interpreted that as you can do all the right things. You can take your family and friends on this amazing adventure, planned to the last degree. You can be extremely patient while everyone around you is catching a fish and still not get the results you want. That's called life. You roll with the punches, and you keep going. Effort is the path to mastery.

Also, celebrate the win. That we did! When we got home, he threw a huge party with all his friends and brought in a caterer so that we could eat his gigantic fish.

Life can give us some messed up circumstances. After all, bad things can (and often do) happen to good people. But good things also happen to good people. So, just like when you catch a big fish, be sure to celebrate the good times and wins in life. Most importantly do it with those you love.

Sure, it is cliché and overused, but it is important for all of us to remember that this is our life to live. You might as well do with it what you want. You are in charge of your own life, so go out and make the most of it! How you show up in the world is the foundation to the farmer's code.

Harvesting

YOU CANNOT SWIM FOR NEW HORIZONS UNTIL YOU
HAVE COURAGE TO LOSE SIGHT OF THE SHORE.

William Faulkner

The Farmer's Code

The hard work and dedication of farmers play an essential role in the provision of food and fiber for our communities and our world. With around-the-clock care, farmers keep humankind nourished and clothed. What would life be like if farmers refused to sell their harvest, selfishly keeping everything they grew to themselves?

If you wanted an apple, you would have to find an apple tree or plant one and wait. If you wanted a new T-shirt, you would have to find the right climate for your cotton plants and learn how to pick those tiny white fluffs out of the sharp husks yourself. Talk about labor intensive! To say nothing of all that work processing and storing the crops so you could have access to the harvest all year. Life would revert back to the dark ages pretty quick if it was every man for himself.

Farmers not only share their harvest, but they also share their knowledge. We are continually seeking new and better ways to increase productivity, reduce costs, and improve sustainability, which drives innovation and research in the agricultural industry. We don't keep discoveries and breakthroughs secret. No! The world is what it is because farmers have always been willing to share their wisdom with others. Their sweat-soaked soil is their legacy.

As Isaac Newton famously said, "If I have seen further, it is by standing on the shoulders of giants." When we are willing to be supportive and share resources, skills, and knowledge with each other, we are, in essence, allowing them to stand on our shoulders. To use our strength as support to achieve their own dreams and goals. This is how we can leave a legacy to those who come behind.

Legacies Are Born from Persistence

Harvest in the life of the farmer represents a culmination of an incredible amount of hard work. It is satisfying to see the fruits of our labor feed the world. Similarly, when we serve others, we experience a sense of purpose and fulfillment for contributing to the well-being and growth of those around us. This is a legacy.

However, there are years when farmers work incredibly hard, but our harvest falls short. Any number of factors beyond our control can reduce yields, despite our best efforts to prevent or mitigate them. The season from 1996 to 1997 was one of those times.

Back then cotton was our family's largest crop in terms of acreage and capital outlay. Cotton is planted in the spring, grown through the hottest parts of the summer, then harvested in the fall. This means you only have a small window of time to plant cotton, so that it grows and matures in time for the harvest before winter storms roll in. The winter of 1996 leading into the spring of 1997 was extremely wet and cold. One of the wettest on record, in fact. The rain was relentless, and soil temperatures at planting were never optimal, so our germinations were very low. Many fields that year were replanted, some twice, in order to get a crop. The late plantings led to a summer that was full of pests, and the heat that year was one for the books. We did everything we possibly could do to protect and nourish our cotton, but no matter what we did, we failed. The bugs kept coming. The temperatures rose. And the plants withered.

The harvest that fall was a disaster. It was a year where we were having to refinance land just to pay back operating expenses. It was one of those years where we struggled just to make payroll. That year was no fun, but it sure did build resiliency.

The experience we had that year is not unlike life. Sometimes you try your absolute best, and you still fail. And that's OK. You don't have to be perfect. As Jean-Luc Picard, the fictional *Star Trek* captain of the starship USS *Enterprise* said in the TV show, "It is possible to commit no mistakes and still lose. That is not a weakness. That is life."

We live in the age of information. I think many of us have become so accustomed to instant access to knowledge that solutions seem like they should be available with no more than a touch of a screen. Do we put forth the same effort to find answers to questions and problems the way previous generations did? Not long ago if a person didn't know the answer to a question or problem, their choices were to find someone smarter than them, find a book, or figure it out themselves. This was just the process of growing up and acquiring knowledge. Nobody expected it to come easy.

Today, I see too many people behave as though they believe they can't solve their own problems. It is almost like they think if they can't find the answers to their questions right away, it is a reflection of them as a person. They get anxious and depressed. They give up. I worry too many of them don't realize that working for knowledge should be a natural part of the learning process and personal growth. And if they get something wrong, it's OK. Sometimes, we actually need to fail for a while.

It's important to remember that failure is not a reflection of our worth as individuals, and it does not define us. Instead, it is an opportunity to learn and grow, and it can ultimately lead us to greater success and fulfillment in our lives. While failing sometimes does come from our mistakes, there are also times when we try our absolute best and still fall short. This can be a really hard place to be in, but it is only through failure that we can learn. The worst thing you can do is give up.

Failure provides an opportunity for reflection, learning, and improvement. It allows us to identify what went wrong, what we can do differently, and how we can move forward. It also helps build resilience and character. When we experience setbacks and difficulties, we develop a better understanding of our strengths and limitations, and we learn to persevere in the face of challenges. This resilience can help us to achieve our goals and overcome obstacles in the future. I am a firm believer that the experience I wrote about earlier from the drunk tank and the failure I was that night to myself and my loved ones clearly opened the door of opportunity for growth.

Moses was so afraid of failure he almost didn't try. Despite being chosen by God to lead the Israelites out of slavery in Egypt, Moses constantly struggled with self-doubt and fear of failure. He was reluctant to accept his calling, citing his inability to speak eloquently as a reason why he couldn't lead the Israelites. He pleaded with God, saying, "O Lord, I'm not very good with words. I never have been, and I'm not now, even though you have spoken to me. I get tongue-tied, and my words get tangled" (Exodus 4:10 NLT).

Because Moses believed he wasn't good at speaking, he was reluctant to accept his calling. God responded that he would make up the difference, and he did by sending Aaron to be his spokesman. When Moses continued to doubt, God said, "What's in your hand?" God isn't looking for a perfect person with a powerful scepter, but only a willing servant gripping a staff. God simply wants to know what you have. Because whatever you have is enough for God to do something miraculous.

Legacies Are Not a Solo Mission

Just as a legacy is not meant to be left for a single person, it cannot be built by a single person either. The key to building a lasting legacy is to include as many people as you can on both sides of the equation. This is not the kind of siloed work we have all become accustomed to in our workplaces and homes. It is, by nature, cooperative and collaborative.

WHATEVER YOU HAVE IS ENOUGH FOR GOD TO DO SOMETHING MIRACULOUS.

I love sports. To me there is no better sporting competition than NCAA's March Madness, the division one basketball tournament that pits sixty-eight of the best college basketball teams in a single elimination tournament with the ultimate winner crowned the national champion. I believe it is the most exhilarating and entertaining time of the year. The intense passion and nail-biting moments of every game make it impossible to look away for even a second. The frenzy of the crowds, the upsets, buzzer beaters, and the Cinderella stories make every minute worth watching.

UCLA basketball coach John Wooden compiled possibly the greatest legacy in college sports history and is considered by many to have been the greatest college coach of all time. From 1964 to 1975, his teams won ten NCAA championships, and, incredibly, his teams won more than six hundred games. That remains an all-time record and is likely to never be broken. Wooden famously said, "The main ingredient to stardom is the rest of the team."

Wooden led by example, showing how much he cared for the team. The basketball team followed him and started working together out of genuine love for one another.

Whether you realize it or not, everything you do has an impact on your community. Even the most antisocial hermit leaves an impression by what they don't do. Maybe they don't appear in public, but their presence is felt when you walk by their home. They exist, and the world knows it. There is no getting away from the fact that you are a part of the world, so I suggest you might as well embrace it.

And then go a step beyond and consider the ripple effect you have on others—or, if you prefer, the wake you will leave behind you. Like a boat traveling across the water, there is a wake behind it that expands exponentially until it reaches the shore. Your wake can be positive or negative or neutral, but it is there. You know what I'm talking about. You smile at the person who checks you out at the grocery store. They smile at the next customer. Who then carries that smile out the door and to the people coming in. Or you scowl, and the same thing happens. It carries on for a long time after you are gone. Like dominoes falling, your energy is contagious.

To create meaningful and lasting impact, it's important to work closely with others as you build relationships of trust. Collaboration is key to solving the complex problems we see today. Seek out partnerships with other people, organizations, and groups who share your goals and can help you achieve them. To strengthen your impact, build networks and coalitions around a common purpose.

Legacies Must Be Passed On

So how do you pass on your legacy? I think this is best illustrated through a story. In junior high I ran track. My mom despised the sport. She would complain, "You drive hours to get to a meet, watch about fifty-five seconds of a race, then drive back home with a sunburned child." I would run the four-by-four-hundred relay. As you probably know, in a relay one member of the team on the track is carrying a baton. As he finishes his leg of the race, he passes the baton to his teammate. This is a crucial part of the race. If the baton is dropped, you lose the race. About the same time I was running track, one of the most storied four-by-one-hundred relay teams of all time was team USA. They were led by Carl Lewis, who at the time was the most decorated Olympic track athlete in history. In the qualifying heat, they dropped the baton and were disqualified from the race. They were not only predicted to win the gold medal, but also to set a world record by a large margin. But instead they lost their chance.

Living and leaving a legacy is all about how you take that baton and successfully pass it to the next generation. Some generations aren't successfully passed a baton, but it's still their responsibility to better what they've been given and pass it on to the next generation. My grandmother was stuck in that situation. She grew up in a family where her father was an alcoholic and abusive. She could have easily taken the baton she was handed of abuse and alcoholism and passed that to the next generation. Instead, she chose something different. She chose love. She chose to walk a different path and successfully pass a baton that she was never given. She couldn't change her past, but she could change her future. She made the decision that she wasn't going to pass on that kind of legacy and, instead, chose to live a different legacy. She chose to take a different path and overcome her upbringing. She chose to pass on love, discipline, and a godly home. She chose a new life, just as Jesus gives us a new life when we give him our heart.

Luke says, "A good man brings good things out of the good stored up in his heart, and an evil man brings evil things out of the evil stored up in his heart. For the mouth speaks what the heart is full of" (Luke 6:45 NIV). The baggage we carry is all right there in our hearts. It's where the wounds and the hurt lie. It easily has the potential to be passed to the next generation. I was fortunate to have learned lessons from my grandmother, grandfather, mom, dad, aunt, and uncle, from the words they spoke to how they handled difficulty, failure, and success. To pass the baton successfully, you have to deal with the things in your heart like unforgiveness, bitterness, anger, lust, fear, greed, and insecurities. You must learn about yourself so you can identify and remove them as they pop up in your life. As you do this, you will become a role model to successfully pass the legacy baton on to the next generation.

Take a moment and think what you are handing off.

Service Is an Obligation

In December 1977, Bakersfield and surrounding areas were hit with a dust storm that lasted three days, leaving five deaths and millions of dollars of damage behind. I was only four years old, and I remember how scared everyone was. Google the pictures. Schools were canceled, and parents had to pick their children up from school because the winds were blowing so hard buses were in danger of being blown over. The power went out, and the sky was blackened with so much dust that even television and radio signals couldn't get through. To make matters worse, news of the disaster didn't reach the outside world until after everything was over, so people heading into town had no idea what they were coming into.

Within twenty-four hours, roads were buried, and every building was filled with a fine layer of dust that had seeped into every crevice. And to add insult to injury, we lost an estimated twenty-five million cubic feet of topsoil because the land was fallow at the time, so it was a huge setback for farmers like my family. My family lived in a house on the ranch at the time. We lost our roof and had to hire men to come and shovel the dirt out of the pool by the wheelbarrow full when it was over.

As crises tend to do, this single event brought out the best in people. A similar dust storm happened in the early 1950s. My grandparents were living on the ranch at the time. GG remembered what it was like. "Our house was built on stilts originally because we lived in a flood plain. Of course they had a curtain around them, but when the storm ended, the sand was level right with the house."

GG remembers many people getting stranded on the country roads during the storm, in some cases cars buried on the roadside from all the blowing dirt. Following the completion of the storm, my grandparents went out to help people who were stranded on the roads. GG made extra coffee, and Grandpa would go out to where people were stuck in the dust and bring it to them. Then he would invite them to come to the house. They never made a big deal of it, because that's what farmers do. They help their neighbors.

We have been born into a time with more advantages and advancements than any other time in history. I believe pretty much every human being on this planet, and particularly in America, has the ability and capacity to serve. I don't care how old, how poor, how uneducated, how busy, or whatever you think you are, service is the reason we were born, because when we are in the service of our fellow human beings, we are actually in the service of our God. Whatever you interpret that God to be.

Service can take many forms, from volunteering at a local charity or community organization to working in a profession that directly serves others, such as healthcare or education. It can be as simple as donating books to a little free library or inviting your neighbor over for dinner. When we engage in service, we are able to connect with others who share similar values and goals and form meaningful relationships that can last a lifetime.

It is imperative to understand that a legacy is not just defined by the accomplishments and material possessions we leave behind, but rather the positive impact we have on others' lives. One of the most significant ways to leave a positive impact on others is through service to them. It is through selfless acts of kindness and support that we bring meaning and purpose to our lives, while simultaneously brightening the lives of others. Service to others fosters a sense of community, instills empathy and compassion, and ultimately creates a ripple effect of positivity that can reach far beyond our physical existence. So, if you want to leave a legacy worth remembering, start by making a difference to those around you today. Live your own version of the farmer's code.

conclusion

THE MEANING OF LIFE IS TO FIND YOUR GIFT.
THE PURPOSE OF LIFE IS TO GIVE IT AWAY.

Chip Conley

Legacy—it's what we stand for and what we want our families to stand for.

I always get a little thrill when I see a family coat of arms or family crest. These may seem like forgotten relics of the past, but when you see one, you can't help but sense its significance. Rich with images like unicorns, lions, flowers, mottos, and weapons, they stand as a reminder of what was most important to a family line. Have you ever stopped to think what you would put on your personal family coat of arms? Would you choose colors that stood for peace or war? Would you choose animals that represented aggression or cooperation? Would your faith, your strength, your wisdom, or your talents be included?

Like a coat of arms, a legacy is a reflection of your values, the things you cherish, the causes you support, and your significance in the world. Legacy building isn't an end-of-life activity; it's something we practice every day. It's not so much about the way you are going to be remembered, but rather how you are going to serve your family, yourself, and your community.

The farmer's code is very much a hero's journey of self-development that takes us on a path of transformation and growth in order to become our true, highest self. Ultimately, to leave a legacy, you've got to dig into yourself, then dig into the relationships you have with others around you. You must go head to head, heart to heart, toe to toe, and face to face with each of those relationships. Head to head means to dig into each relationship intentionally. Heart to heart means to love each relationship unconditionally. Toe to toe means to constructively challenge each relationship to grow and thrive. Then face to face means to look each relationship square in the eye so that they know you are there for them and that you are both in it together.

This journey can sometimes be accompanied by personal struggles, often featuring physical, psychological, and spiritual elements that must be overcome, but it will always lead to a greater understanding of the self and a deeper connection to our own values and core principles.

As my grandmother continues to thrive after more than a century of life, I think about how I would have curated my life differently if, in my early twenties, I knew I was going to live past one hundred.

The farmer's code is about living a legacy rather than just leaving one. If we are living it on the daily, then we will certainly be able to smoothly pass that baton to the future. It is about being committed to something bigger than ourselves, just as God intended and Jesus taught.

Living and leaving a legacy means it's not about us. It means giving to others and living like it isn't even our life, just as Jesus did when he walked the earth. Jesus changed others because he only thought of them, not himself. Living a legacy is all about love.

Love does. Love gives. Love unites. Love is the key to leaving legacies. As my grandmother GG said, "Why do I think this family is so special? Because of our sacrificial love!" Sacrificial love changes the world.

The farmer's code is all about legacy building. It is not just about overcoming obstacles and rising above challenges; it is about leaving a mark that lasts beyond our lifetime. As you embark on your journey, you acquire new skills and knowledge that you can pass down to future generations. Your actions will inspire others to follow in your footsteps and continue your work. With that you will establish a reputation and a legend that will be retold for years to come, ensuring that your impact is felt long after you are gone. The farmer's code, therefore, is not only a personal journey but a means to build a lasting legacy and contribute to the world in a meaningful way.

LOVE DOES. LOVE GIVES. LOVE UNITES. LOVE IS THE KEY TO LEAVING LEGACIES.

Now go and enjoy the journey. Live your own farmer's code.